THE GOLFING MIND

THE
GOLFING
MIND

*The Psychological
Principles of Good Golf*

ROBERT A. BROWN, Ph. D.

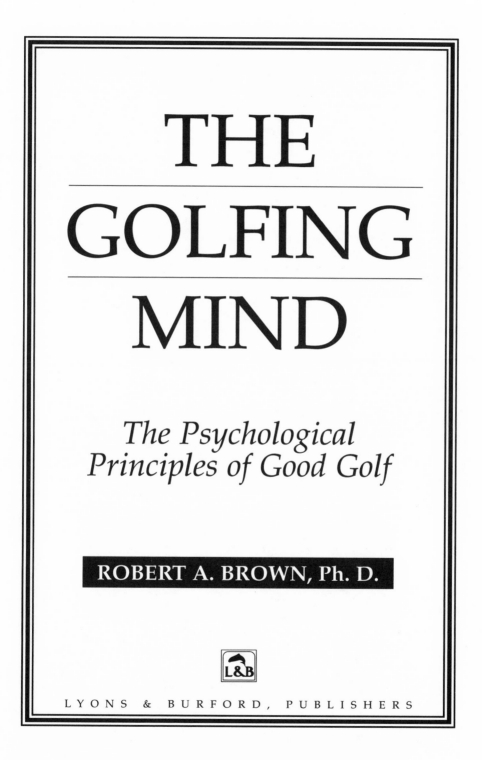

L Y O N S & B U R F O R D , P U B L I S H E R S

Printed in the United States of America

Design by Howard P. Johnson

10 9 8 7 6 5 4 3 2

Library of Congress Cataloging-in-Publication Data

Brown, Robert A. (Robert Alexander), 1946-
    The golfing mind: the psychological principles of good golf / Robert A. Brown.
        p. cm.
    Includes bibliographical references and index.
    ISBN 1-55821-294-9 (cloth); ISBN 1-55821-439-9 (paperback)
    1. Golf—Psychological aspects.
GV979.P75B76   1994
796'.01" 9—dc20   94-12731
                                                CIP

THIS BOOK IS DEDICATED TO THE OTHER GUYS IN THE FOURSOME ON MARCH 13, 1989; JIM HAY, BRENT MAYNARD AND NICK COLOVUS.

ACKNOWLEDGMENTS
IX
INTRODUCTION
XI

ACKNOWLEDGMENTS

I thank my wife Deena and two wonderful kids, Denelle, who is bright and beautiful, and Rob, who is handsome and intelligent, and my father-in-law Jim Williams who offered much to the manuscript.

I am grateful for the support of Dr. Farrally, John I. C. Scott, Ann Campbell and Nigel Mayglothling (now back in England), of the Physical Education department of St Andrews University, Scotland, where, as an Honourary Reader, I was able to complete this project. Although I am responsible for any oversights, the following friends have made this book much better than it otherwise would have been. My thanks to:

Martin Farrally, Ph.D., St Andrews University

Jim Rhoads, J.D., The San Diego Golf Academy

Jill Prolman, Ph.D., Encinitas, California

Doug Hoffmann, PGA, Casselberry, Florida

Dennis Blakeslee, Ph.D., Scripps Clinic, California

Conrad Rehling, PGA, University of Alabama

Gene Smith, PGA, Orlando, Florida

Sharon Colgan, Ph.D., San Diego, California

And a salute to some of my direct and indirect mentors, Bob Carrie, Chuck Hogan, Bruce Ogilvie, Vivien Saunders, Gary Wiren, Dick Coop, Roger Kaufman, Bob Rotella and Linda Bunker.

INTRODUCTION

The mental aspects of golf are as old as the game itself. Concentrating on a tough chip, anguishing over a missed shot, mulling over the day's play have been with us from the very beginning. New, however, is the scientific study of human behavior, developed primarily during the last one hundred years. The science of psychology is crowded with many theories, each claiming to best portray how we think and why we do the things we do. What is even younger, still in its infancy, is sports psychology, the application of the science of human behavior to maximizing athletic performance.

What the players of old did automatically, with methods and skills developed through trial and error, modern sports psychology is now attempting to distil. The idea is to understand what experts seem to acquire naturally, so that all golfers can benefit from the learning experiences of the finest players. I have done my best to summarize what I think is the basic psychological knowledge that is necessary for understanding the mental fundamentals of golf.

I have tried to cover the areas of psychology that are germane to golf and translate them into concepts the serious player can use. The first section on the psychological theories that apply to golf is somewhat technical and seemingly far removed from swinging a club at the ball. Although complicated, understanding these concepts will make the rest of the mental game much easier. Acquiring a good mental game is like learning the swing: You might suffer a few mental blisters and cramps along the way, but you will be well rewarded for your efforts.

I hope that the wisdom of the shepherds, the canny play of the old Scots and the science of the modern professionals are all presented to your advantage. Good luck.

THE GAME

This book is for the golfer who seriously wants to improve, the competitive golfer who wants to squeeze that last bit from his game and the weekend player who is seeking to increase his enjoyment and be more confident, less frustrated, more forgiving and more deadly with those six-foot putts. At any skill level, most golfers can gain significant benefit from the new science and the old wisdom that is the mental game.

The mental game is not a set of techniques to be applied whenever certain situations occur, like relaxing with deep breathing if you sense growing tension. That's like always chipping with a wedge whenever you're just off the green. Sometimes that's the right club, other times not. The best players know when to use an 8-iron or even a 5-iron instead. Those most adept at golf know how to accurately identify the relevant problem and how to create the best solution. True knowledge in the mental game is achieved when the player knows how to adjust to the always-changing conditions of the course, the game and himself.

A good mental game is independent of ability and can be defined as a special kind of self-awareness that enables the player to apply his physical skills and his thought processes with minimal interference from personal weaknesses and external conditions. The golfer with a good mental game knows how to identify and define problems, how to design personal strategies to deal with these problems without distraction from the outside, and how to create a response that best suits his own abilities. Let's start our investigation into the fundamentals with a couple of examples of the golfing mind.

Beginning golfer Rich has a 150-yard shot to the green. His friend Dave, a good player, has a similar shot and has just told Rich that he thinks a 7-iron will get him there. If Rich had no mental game whatsoever, he would pull out a 7-iron too and swing away, coming up short ninety-nine percent of the time. But Rich has a mental game. He wants to hit the ball as far as Dave but knows that he can't. He also knows that his shot could fly at the stick, sail into the water behind the green or roll fifty feet with almost equal probability. He sets up with one goal in mind: put a good swing on the ball with his 6-iron and accept whatever happens. This is a good mental game.

Susan, on the other hand, is a good college golfer with aspirations of competing on the LPGA tour. On another course at another time, she, too, has 150 yards to the green. This approach and a two-putt par would give her a tie for the tournament championship. She relishes this first chance at a title. Her heart pounds as she anxiously sorts out her options: go for the center of the green and safety, or try for the outright win. Although she has fantasized about this situation a million times, she never realized that her palms could be so sweaty or her shirt collar feel so tight.

Susan also has a good mental game. She holds onto her bag as she begins a slow breathing technique designed to calm her down. When she feels ready, she decides that her goal is to hit at the flag, ready to rely on her short game if she misses right.

After two more deep breaths, she chooses her 8-iron, aware that she is pumped up, and methodically goes through her preshot routine. Just when she is ready to hit, a car horn distracts her. She

2

steps back, acknowledges to herself that she is ready, reminds herself that she has made this shot hundreds of times, repeats her preshot routine slowly and smoothly as always and busts her 8-iron to within three feet.

The mental game cannot make a good golf swing. Susan had to practice a lot to be able to play at the tournament level. Rich will have to play many more rounds and have a few more lessons before he can get rid of his frustrating banana ball. What the mental game *can* do is get your best swing to the course. Susan has the swing and only has to get out of her own way. Rich needs to relax so he can let his hands release through the ball.

PERCEPTION, PROCESSING AND PERFORMING

There are three psychological elements that make up the mental game: the various ways your mind perceives a situation, how it processes that information, and how it stimulates the body to perform. Problems can, and certainly do, occur in each of these areas. Unless problems can be accurately defined, they cannot be solved, and in golf there are always two sets of problems: the physical ones of hitting the ball to the right place and the mental ones of getting ready to do that. Most golfers define only the physical ones and ignore the mental. Physically, a 150-yard shot is easy to define—the lie of the ball, the wind, the slope and so on. Psychologically, however, a 150-yard shot is much more complicated. For beginner Rich, the psychological demands of a 150-yard approach shot might be a number of things:

1. A chance to prove his skill
2. A shot too difficult for him
3. The easiest chance so far at a par
4. A fun shot with his favorite club
5. Intense desire to follow Dave's good shot with one equally good
6. Another chance of a slice
7. Etc.

3

Defining the problem is the first step in perceiving. Rich's perception of the possible emotional meaning of that 150 yards is an additional problem beyond simply hitting the ball the right distance.

The second element in the mental game is processing information. Assessing distance and wind direction is the easy part. The difficult portion is self-awareness, which is knowing ourselves and our tendencies and making both rational and emotional decisions at the same time. Many poor shots are not caused by the body's making a mistake but are the result of the player's doing exactly what his mind wanted him to do. Saying to yourself "Don't go right," actually increases the chance of a mishit, either to the right or in some other way. There is a good reason for this which we will discuss later. The mental game can help you know what dangers lurk both on the course and in your mind.

The simplest and easiest element of the mental game is swinging the club. Basically, the thinking mind has to get out of the way and let the body do what it has been trained to do. The problem here is that often the mind has the body too scared to do its job or too misdirected to be at all coordinated. The golf swing is a complicated series of movements that, once learned, **do not require thoughtful guidance**. But it is difficult to let the body have a seemingly uncontrolled swing at the ball when a championship is riding on the outcome. It doesn't feel right to turn off our brains when staying in control is critical. But this is part of the mental game too. Being able to analyze complex problems, make courageous decisions, and then turn off the thinking process is the mental game. The mental game is also being aware of how thinking itself can cause its own set of problems such as overanalysis, faulty assumptions and irrational decision making.

The mental game is a combination of thoughts and feelings, physical reactions to anxiety and fears, and course management. For example, John, a college player, was invited to the Masters Golf Tournament, thanks to his match-play win in the U.S. Amateur. He tried to pretend that it was just another tournament in order to cope with the tremendous tension of playing the Augusta National course and in his first professional Major. He played two practice rounds and shot 72, 71. His two tournament rounds in front of crowds larger than the population of his home town were 83, 88. His golf swing was fine, but his brain couldn't cope with all the new

4

experiences. Since he did not create an effective mental game, John had to follow the weekend play from outside the ropes.

Your personality and the way you think are just as much a part of your golf swing as your coordination. In fact, your ability to concentrate is probably more important to your golf game than something as basic as your grip. Yet how much time do you take to work on improving your concentration, as compared to making sure your grip is okay? Is your concentration as good as it can be? Do you even know *how* to improve your concentration?

THE MENTAL COURSE

Assume for a moment that your mind is like a golf course. Since you use it everyday, like a course you have played a thousand times, it feels like you know it well. Believe me, you don't.

Your mental "course" changes all the time, sometimes in seconds. What was easy last week is impossible today. Confidence ebbs and flows, "momentum" shifts in an instant. A missed ten-footer can intensify your determination or break your heart. To play your best golf, you must be aware of what this internal golf course is all about and how to manage its strengths and hazards.

We will explore the complexities of the mental game by first investigating some of the general characteristics of golfers and then by looking at how the brain and mind work. A little knowledge of how your brain and mind operate can save you a lot of trouble when you read other mental game material and when you apply techniques on the course. Most other sources of the mental game tend to give you specific advice on what to do. This book has been designed to give you general information so you can decide what changes to make in practice and in play, based upon what works for you.

5

‖‖‖

THE PLAYERS

Golf is a game of many levels, from junior golfers racing around par 3 courses, to championships chased by professionals over 7,000-yard monsters, to seniors playing for nickels around the putting green outside the recreation center. What makes golf unique is how the game can stretch the ability of the best, and shrink to be enjoyed by the young, the inexperienced, the inept, the blind, the physically disabled, the old, the weak—everybody. Because of the nature of golf, and the nature of man, everyone can play golf, and anyone can compete against anyone else. More so in golf than most other games, however, the player also competes against himself.

As we know, the mental game is a complicated combination of thoughts, emotions and beliefs. Put together what goes on in the mind with the demands of the golf course and it is difficult to sort out if the game is hard or if the player's mind is creating most of the problems. Is the course really knocking us around or are we "psyched out" by its reputation or by the craftiness of the architect? What makes grown adults cringe over four-foot putts and fear like the plague a little sand and water? This chapter investigates the golfer and his mental approach to the course, as well as the course and its effect on the player. We will begin with a short story about Stanley, a good golfer gone slightly off kilter. He has read all the books, subscribed to all the magazines, tried all the gadgets and still wants to quit the game every Sunday night. Stanley's a golf nut; his mind, however, works very much like yours and mine.

THE GENERIC GOLFER

Three days of nonstop rain had dampened the enthusiasm of even the most avid golfers. All the members sat sullenly about the club, frustrated that there was no longer any reason to put off going home to long-abandoned chores. All, that is, except young Stan Emerson. With great purpose he marched about the clubhouse, to and fro in front of the view window, loudly complaining about the injustice of it all. "I had it figured out. That last lesson was the key. It's just not fair! I know how to play. Today was the day . . . I know today could have been the day!"

Back and forth he went, gazing all the while out to the first tee, which, by the way, could scarcely be seen through the downpour.

"Just a simple adjustment, that's all there was. . . ."

He became more agitated as he fruitlessly searched the sky for any sign of blue, or even just a slight letup so the course could reopen. But no, as if to torment him alone, the sky darkened and the rain fell even harder into the deeply soaked earth.

With the despair experienced only by golfers on a day when it is truly impossible to play, he drove home through mocking puddles and a following wind that would have enabled him to reach number 6 in two strokes. Within minutes of his arrival, and subsequent fruitless meanderings around the garage, his wife came out with a steaming-hot cup of coffee and some sound, if maybe brutally direct, advice.

7

"You should have your head examined," she said, "all this carrying on about golf. You've had a million lessons and they haven't worked." Then, with the compassion only a golf widow can summon, she added, "Why don't you schedule an appointment with Professor Vatson, the sports psychologist at the university? He could get your game back on track."

Stanley, wanting no stone left unturned, went to get his head examined, and on the next Saturday morning met Dr. Jackson Vatson, who looked curiously like old Tom Morris. He explained his turmoil with his game and his fruitless search for improvement. He went on to describe his thoughts on golf and the comments of the many professionals he had consulted.

After Stanley completed his summary, the Professor inquired, "You are a golf player, correkt?"

"Yes, yes. That is what I have been trying to explain," Stanley answered, now aware that the Professor couldn't tell a 5- iron from a water ball.

"Vat you haf iz ein problem mit der approach-avoidance complex. Und golf player should vant to approach und avoid both at ze same time. You however, haf ze problem; too much approach und zen you vant to avoid.

"Huh?"

"Let me make you example. Young man sees young lady at svimming pool. He vants uff course to impress her, und decides to dive off high tower. He approaches ze tower, mit love in his heart und bounce in his step. Climbs higher und higher, den realizes he could get himself kilt. Vanting to avoid zat, he comes down und down until he sees clearly ze young lady again und his heart leaps und up he goes again. Up und down und up und down he goes. Finally he stops, haffvay up der ladder. Young man izt stuck until somethink can help him make up hist mind for vat to do. Dot izt you. Undershtant?"

"Well . . . actually, no."

"Oh. So sorry." Waving his hand, the professor ushered Stanley to the door, "Time izt finished. Ve talk again maybe."

Walking out, Stanley suddenly realized what the professor's approach-avoidance complex was all about. "Of course," he thought, "the approach part is that I love the game and really want to play well. Then I try too hard and lose all the fun. Then I want to avoid the frustration and don't try anymore, which takes the pressure off making me want to play; but if I don't try, then I lose the fun all over again. First I have too much approach, then too much avoidance, then not enough approach. I have to find the balance between approach and avoidance to keep it fun and exciting. The more approach AND avoidance, the greater the tension and excitement.

"Oh boy. I've got it now," he said on the drive home, which included a very successful detour for a quick nine at the club. Stanley realized that some degree of hesitation, of uncertainty, was necessary to create the right kind of excitement, but not too much or too little. For poorer players, there is enough uncertainty in the swing alone. For better players, the tension balance is created by the mental demands of higher expectations, competition, and the search for improvement.

Stanley's quest for a good golf swing had to include his mental approach and an understanding of the demands of the golf course. An important part of that search had to be inside himself— for a sense of satisfaction, of accomplishment, and a little fun. Much of the difficulty of golf is how our minds formulate the internal approach-avoidance conflict. What the professionals call "a burning in the belly" prior to tournament play is a strongly felt approach-avoidance tension. We can all feel it to varying degrees in different situations. Even a "course" as simple as a driving range can be a difficult and interesting challenge if we ask ourselves to hit five consecutive wedges to a brown spot a hundred yards away with dire consequences if we fail.

APPROACH-AVOIDANCE

In 1993, Chip Beck, the world-class optimist, faced a very public and very intense approach-avoidance conflict when he reached his tee shot on the par-5 15th hole at the Masters. Trailing Bernhard Langer by three strokes at the time, he was just outside the distance at which his decision would be automatic. On the next page is how going for the green in two might have been categorized in his mind.

These and a lot of other concerns were rushing through Beck's mind at the time. He had to decide with some measuring device which of the many thoughts he should pay attention to. Some per-

9

APPROACH	AVOIDANCE
Great chance to pick up a stroke	*Could give it all away here*
Put some heat on Bernhard	*Outside comfortable range*
Pump me up	*Look foolhardy if not successful*
Want to win	*Birdie might pick up one stroke*
	anyway
	Kick myself for blowing it
	Miss might affect second place
	Requires perfect stroke
	Don't want to lose

sonalities, like a Lanny Wadkins, would pull out the big stick. Nowhere on their avoidance list is fear of failure. Not going full out would be what they would avoid. Beck's thoughtful decision was to continue to play the percentages. There was no need for him to give away the title, and not enough chance of benefit to try a big move at that time.

Naturally, he was faulted for his decision to lay up. Going for it would have been heroic. Notice that nowhere on his approach list was being heroic. For someone else's list, like a Wadkins or a Calcavecchia, that may have been part of the decision. Not for Beck. Bad decisions are made all the time, and not just in sports, by having the wrong kind of items on your approach-avoidance list, and making the decision based more on the list than the situation. As you will learn, the golf course provides only part of the hazards and difficulties of golf. Our assumptions, needs, values and a whole host of other mental factors come into play.

THE FIVE-MILE COURSE

The mind seeks a challenge and at the same time attempts to create harmony. The real-world golf course, with its fairways, roughs, bunkers, greens, out-of-bounds, side hills, wind and whatever, says to the golfer, "Here I am, do your best." A golf hole or course can be designed to be a number of things, from an easy, relaxing walk in a park to a demoralizing and punitive day-long struggle. The physical reality of a golf course initiates the mental processes.

The basic measure of the interest and challenge of a golf

course or a particular hole is its shot values, that is, the attainability of par and the hurdles or obstacles that exist in reaching it. A short hole with no bunkering has poor shot values because it is too easy, while a long uphill par-4 with water on both sides of a narrow fairway can be faulted for being too difficult. As far as the mental game goes, neither stimulates much of an approach-avoidance tension in the golfer. An easy hole produces no avoidance in the poor golfer and little approach in the good player, while an overly difficult hole creates too much avoidance in both players. (However, any hole can change its character in an instant when the wind picks up, if your match-play opponent has just hit his tee shot out of bounds, or you need a par to win the club championship.) A good golf hole is one that interests all levels of golfers and makes each one think and execute to his own level of ability in order to enjoy success. For this reason, a hole is designed as a problem to be solved by an accurate assessment of its demands, a realistic appraisal of the players' abilities and the application of physical skill. The golf course only initiates the mental challenge. Inside the mind of the player are even more obstacles to identify and overcome.

THE SIX-INCH COURSE

Beginners' minds have little available space and time for the details and variations of the golf swing, the kind of knowledge that must be considered on the course. The driving range is a difficult enough venue for them at first. Their focus should be on swing cues and on enjoying the process of learning and mastery. But anything that is too easy soon becomes boring. As a player develops skills, he seeks increasingly greater challenges in order to continue his interest in the game. This is the mind at work. The ego actually defines easy victories as negative.

The six-inch course between your ears is similar to a 7,000-yard one in that it has a goal, obstacles and ways of getting from point A to point B. The goal, or par, of the mental course is not to get into the hole in the fewest number of strokes but to feel a sense of control and competence, to comprehend, to minimize anxiety and to feel success. Par in the mental game is relative, defined by the player, just like bogey is a relative par on the course for a nineties shooter.

11

Let's take a look at two different kinds of players, the one who plays for fun and maybe a buck or two, and the player who makes a living at the game. Both have the same components of human nature and mental activities that we will discuss later. What information they take in is very different, but how they process it is the same and the mental goals and obstacles are very similar.

THE WEEKEND PLAYER

The mental par for a weekend player is fun. However that par is individually defined, the weekend player seeks some kind of enjoyment when he plays. For most, this means that golf has to be different from work. Practicing is work, not fun, which is why most players don't go to the range. Reading about golf is fun, and so is reading a golf tip that is easy to apply. Buying new equipment is fun, especially buying a club that promises more distance, which means a lot more fun.

Playing with your friends is fun. Winning a small wager is fun. Playing the back tees at a championship course and getting beaten up is fun. Playing a beautiful and easy resort course and recording your best score ever is fun.

Immediate fun can be sacrificed if satisfaction is achieved after the round. "The worst round I ever played," horrible at the time, can be fun to talk about at the 19th hole. Fun is the goal, the difficulty of the game the obstacle and just the right balance of seriousness and relaxation the method used by weekend players to reach that goal. For example, the amount of the wager keeps the interest (the right balance of approach-avoidance), but does not make the game overly serious for the weekend player. Traditionally, the winner buys the drinks, which evens things out anyway.

As Johnny Miller has often stated, it is a good idea to have a lot of arrows in the quiver. The weekend golfer, in his pursuit of fun, has lots of ways to do it: a little wager for a prize, one miracle shot over a pond or under a tree branch, one spectacular disaster, the successful use of a new, unpracticed technique, a few good holes, breaking ninety, not trying overly hard, reaching for the all-time long drive and feeling a little pleasant muscle fatigue in spite of a string of triple bogeys. Experiencing any one of these can make the outing fun.

The mind of the golfer who plays for fun should recognize that goal and use mental techniques to enhance his pleasure first, and his golf score second.

THE PROFESSIONAL

The professional, psychologically, aims his arrows at only one target. If one phrase can be used to describe the approach of a professional golfer, it is "single-mindedness." The professional's drive to compete and win is his single defining characteristic. The amateurs who are driven to win the club tournament or the Saturday Nassau are like professionals in their approach, again defined by the single-minded drive to perform well. If you are a competitor, then you must keep in mind that your self-esteem is at risk each time you play. You are not out for fun, even though competition can be enjoyable and satisfying. As far as your ego is concerned, you do not have nearly the number of arrows that the fun loving weekender has. The mental game fundamental for the competitor is to put self-esteem at risk, and keep it at risk, no matter how poorly the game is going. Often the competitor creates more of a problem by believing that there is only one way to define success: a lower score, in comparison with the field or his opponent.

The mind of the professional must learn to overcome the natural tendencies to avoid risk, to run when threatened, to react too quickly when anxious and to try too hard when the reward is so very important. The mental game for the professional must foster a good swing and protect self-esteem at the same time. Awareness of how the brain and mind work is as important for the professional as knowing the loft and lie of his clubs. Knowing the effect of personality factors and information processing is as important to success nowadays as knowing how to swing.

The competitive player must be single-minded, which means that adversity, bad luck, more skillful opponents or breathing the rarefied air of finding yourself within reach of a major championship do not become obstacles. A reaction to any distraction is in itself another distraction from winning. It is not that you must be single-minded to succeed. Many successful champions are not at all single-minded in their daily living. But you must be able to become single-minded while competing. That will not be easy, as you will learn in the next few chapters.

Although the mind of the average golfer who plays for fun and that of the professional work in the same way, the kind of information processed, the intensity of the goals and obstacles, and the damage from the risks and the response to the risks are different. We will talk a lot about decision-making, goal-setting and comfort zones in later chapters. Make sure as you look at the material that you are well aware of what you want, what is in your way, both in your own mind and in the nature of the game, and how to use mental techniques to get where you want to go.

THE BASICS

en thousand thousand years ago, before old Tom Morris sank his first putt, before a shepherd absentmindedly swung his crook at a loose stone, long before games were invented, the mind of the modern golfer was being formed.

The efforts made by our primitive forebears to hunt and gather, to mate, fight, survive and make sense of their world required physical effort and, increasingly, intelligent problem-solving. Learning to throw a stone blended the insight of using tools with the coordination of a finely tuned body. We haven't changed much. Physically, we have become taller, healthier and in many ways stronger than the early hunters. Mentally, we are smarter, and our instincts and emotions are less controlling. But, even though our brain capacity is much larger, the way we process information is similar to that of our ancestors. We still have old and sometimes destructive tendencies.

Modern man has learned a considerable amount about how the body works, especially in the last hundred years. From medicine and biomechanics to nutrition and biophysics, all of us, and especially the modern athlete, have gained a continually increasing ability to enhance physical efforts, whether to survive pneumonia, to pilot a spaceship or to drive a golf ball three hundred yards. With the rise of video techniques, the fundamentals of the golf swing have become very well understood. The mental fundamentals are a little more elusive.

Observing professional golfers, one can see the number of very different but equally effective swings these players have. Each player has created a swing that is best suited to his particular body type, physical strengths and weaknesses and emotional temperament. Although there does seem to be an ideal body type, grip, swing plane, swing arc, etc., since no one is identical to anyone else, the combination of these physical basics has to be customized by the individual. The end result, of course, is a functional golf swing. The same is true for the mental game. There are a few standard concepts like relaxation and concentration, but the needs of the individual player and the methods of putting his ideas into practice are specific to each player.

THE MENTAL FUNDAMENTALS OF GOLF

Every golfer is aware of some of the mental fundamentals. Confidence and concentrating on one swing at a time are the keys for all of us. Unfortunately, we all have our common negative fundamentals too. We swing harder than we should when upset or angry, for example, or we get nervous over a tough putt when it may mean the loss of a match. Most players rightly assume that these experiences are normal emotional responses and a normal part of golf. No big deal. Who needs to study what is normal everyday stuff? The players who just tee it up and "let 'er rip" are exercising their right to play their own game. However, these folks, knowingly or not, are limiting their improvement to whatever they may learn on the

16

course, and by whatever their particular natural physical and mental limits happen to be. They are not reading this book, nor will they play their best.

There is another kind of player who is actually a golfer rather than just someone who plays golf. This individual subscribes to magazines and buys books on golf technique and may even have a text on the mental game, but if so, it was probably a gift. This person believes that things you can touch and change are real, while the thinking process is either something you have or don't have, or something too unfamiliar or too weird to try to fool around with.

The highest form of golfer is the "player," the one who skillfully applies his swing to the ball, and with clear thinking seeks and learns realistic and productive methods. He may be a low handicap or high. His major skill is his practical and artistic approach to the game. Let the "player" in you be your guide as you read this book. As we explore the complicated details of the mental game, make sure you understand each concept so that you can appreciate the reason for the techniques we discuss. I want you to learn enough about mental concepts and techniques so you can solve problems and repair your own mental game as needed out on the course. Let me show you an example of how the mental aspects can be simple, subtle and destructive. Keep in mind that this example is about someone who plays at the highest level and should know all about the mental game.

THE EXPERT

Nick is in his seventh season on the American PGA Tour. With four wins he was not quite a star, but he was on the way up and seriously thinking about the possibilities of winning a Major. He played quick and he took dead aim at the pins. Nick's attitude was like an Old West gunslinger—go for broke, make it happen, never back down. Fans loved his style and now it is only a matter of time before he makes it really big.

We catch up with him on the 8th hole during the second round of the PGA Championship. Although the birdie putts aren't dropping, he is just six strokes off a very hot pace. Only a dozen players are between him and the top spot. His even-par round is not what he needs, and Nick is doing what he can to make something happen. This six-foot birdie putt is where he intends to turn it around.

In his usual style, he stalks around the edge of the green while waiting for his playing companions to putt out. Now his turn, he places his ball with the name behind and slightly up as a target and a reminder to hit through to the hole. His patented quick jab pulls the ball just a hair and it stops six inches past. Mentally kicking himself for missing such an easy chance, he backhands the ball, and misses again.

One stroke has been given away, but Nick is a pro and he regroups, eventually finishing the tournament in the top fifteen. This lapse of concentration—or maybe it was simply discharging built-up frustration—was clearly a mental error and an obvious loss of a stroke. It was just as obvious a mistake as overclubbing or mis-judging the wind. But was it?

From a psychological perspective, it wasn't a mistake at all. Nick was exasperated at missing so many birdie chances during the front nine that another one was more than his pride could stand. He was angry at the course and expressed his irritation by ignoring it for a moment. No concentration on the short putt was his way of saying, "You stupid course, I'll just get my quick par and get off your stupid green."

> **Nick was actually meeting a psychological need that was more important to him than making the short par putt.**

Of course he wanted to make the putt, but his expression of irritation, partly to himself, partly to the course and partly to the gallery, temporarily was a more important goal than going through his usual putting routine or making the putt.

Your mental game is not just another part of playing golf. It is primarily a vehicle for meeting your emotional needs and often does so at the expense of your performance. Sometimes the mental game is as apparent as angrily missing a gimmie, but most often it steals half a stroke here and there, or slowly but surely wears down emotional energy over the course of a round or the tournament.

18

THE BEGINNER

Since we were all beginners at one time, I'll describe a few more aspects of the mental game through the experience of a student new to golf. This section might be of special interest to teachers.

On a warm spring morning our excited neophyte Judi arrives at the course with a brand-new starter set and a considerable amount of apprehension. She has heard how difficult the game is from her long-suffering husband, an average weekend player who returns home in a variety of moods after playing golf. It was he who suggested that she take up the game.

Although he never had a lesson himself, her husband knew the wisdom of a good beginning and the folly of his attempting to teach her. Perhaps his wisest decision in golf was to arrange Judi's start with a professional. The club pro, Don, has years of experience as a player and a teacher. He greets her on the practice tee.

"Good morning, Judi. Ready to start?"

"Hi, Don. Well, I'm kinda nervous," she says with a little laugh.

"That's to be expected. Just relax and we'll have a good time. Why don't you take out your 7-iron and we'll start with the basics?"

So far, readers, Don has only made one error with the mental game. Not bad considering he spoke five whole sentences.

"Judi, your grip looks real good. Has your husband been working with you?"

"A little. He wanted me to know some things before I really got started."

"Good. Now let's see your stance."

Mistake number two.

"Super. Your stance is real good too. Now take a few swings. Great. Wow, you have a ton of natural talent!"

Error number three.

"Thanks," says Judi, feeling a little more confident.

"Hit a few balls. Don't worry where they go."

Mistake number four.

Judi proceeds to top the first half-dozen or so, slice a few, top, hit a good one, top, top—you know how it goes. As the lesson continues, Don wisely makes only a few suggestions. The most important advice is for Judi to shift her weight more on the downswing.

19

"Well, Judi, you're off to a good start. Not many balls in the air, but that's okay. What's important is that you're enjoying yourself and getting solid basics."

Don was excited about her potential and told her so. It didn't matter, he said, that few balls were hit well that first time. That was normal. The game takes a while to learn. Judi, however, went home unhappy.

Let's analyze what happened from a psychological point of view. First, Don noticed that Judi was a little nervous and suggested that she relax and enjoy the lesson. Noticing the anxiety was a plus; telling her to relax was completely useless except perhaps to make Don feel he was doing a good job. The part of the brain that controls emotions and the part that thinks are not connected in such a way that you can easily convince yourself to relax. If they were, I'd be out of a job.

Don's second error was in disregarding Judi's admission that her husband had taught her a few things. What did he teach her? Was it good advice or something that might prove to be counterproductive? For example, Judi's husband might have told her that Don was the best teacher in the world and was especially successful with helping beginners. That would be good, and good for Don to know. Or, she could have been told that Don was the best teacher in the world and she was lucky that a lesson could be arranged with him because he worked only with the best. This was actually the case and the reason Judi already had worked on the grip and stance with her husband. Judi was anxious about meeting her husband's and her new teacher's expectations.

Don made a third error in telling her that she had a ton of talent. Judi was a successful athlete and confirmation that she had talent caused her to raise both her confidence and her expectations. As we will discover, expectations and frustration are sister and brother, in a constant state of sibling rivalry.

Judi and Don made a fourth error which resulted in her leaving the lesson and deciding that she would not be back. Judi's specific expectations weren't met. She did not finish the lesson able to hit the ball in the air. Don did not make sure he knew exactly what she wanted out of the lesson. Judi, a gifted tennis player and former softball league batting champ, had seen her husband hit the ball in the air, had seen the players on TV easily hit the ball high and incredibly far every time and had been told by her friends how great it was

20

to watch the ball arch high in the sky and then fall gently on target. Further, adding insult to injury, his reference to weight shift accidentally focused on the ten extra pounds she was hoping to ignore. Already trying to cope with other signs of approaching middle age, this affront to her fading youth was too distressing for her to tolerate. She quit.

Don did not address her expectations. Had he done so, he might have been able to help her redefine her goals into ones that were more attainable and enjoyable. Both Judi and Don missed the importance of her expectations. Each perceived the situation differently: Judi was aware of how hard it was to hold the club, stand in that uncomfortable way and swoop at the tiny ball only to hit the top of it and watch it bounce along the grass. Don's eyes saw a new but coordinated player respond to instruction and miss hitting successful shots by only a fraction. He was excited at the potential of a strong, coordinated woman out enjoying the wonderful game of golf. Judi defined the situation as futile efforts by a frumpy has-been.

Judi's expectations were as fundamental to her first golf lesson as the grip, perhaps even more so. With a faulty grip, she could still learn and play, but without appropriate expectations, she never made it to the course. Judi's perceptions were not the same as Don's, nor were her definitions of what she perceived. Had she been able to judge her swing in the same way as Don did, maybe her expectations could have been met. Don didn't do a bad job. He just didn't look beyond swing mechanics to Judi's mental needs. Who could know that Judi was worried about other people's expectations and her own declining abilities? The answer is that Don could have.

As for Nick, the Tour player, he continued on with his play at the PGA Championship aware that his mental lapse caused the loss of a stroke and handled it like the competitor he is. What he didn't realize was that other areas of his mental game added a total of five more lost strokes, the difference between an outright win and his top-fifteen finish.

Nick, Judi and Don are intelligent and sensitive people and don't always make mental errors, but too often do from simple lack of information or faulty thinking. My assumption in this book is that you are doing the same thing. Sometimes a logical approach to golf does not take into account the cognitive and emotional factors that are *always* present.

21

The mental game is not a mystery. But it does require a different way of defining the situation and a different way of making things happen. We all have enjoyed the power of the mind on occasion. When you know a putt will drop before you hit it, when you take a 6 when it's really 5-iron distance and knock it stiff, when you hesitate over a shot, the mental game is in action. Now is the time to learn it well enough to get it under your control.

THE GOLFER AS HUMAN BEING

Is golf really "ninety percent mental?" I don't know, but I'll tell you what I think and you can make up your own mind. As I said earlier, the mental fundamentals are made up of varying items depending on what level is being discussed. Popular topics today in the mental game are attitude and attention. Although important, this level of definition is not enough to help us understand the fundamentals. How much would it help your game if a teacher came to you and said, "I know what your problem is. You have a bad attitude. Think more positive."? This helps as much as being told to get a better swing when the ball is going off line.

What can you do to improve a negative attitude? The answer is the same for a flaw in your swing: It depends. For a bad swing, a good teacher would determine what specific areas of your swing didn't work, evaluate your abilities and then put together a plan for improvement. Same with the mental game. You, as the golfer, or your teacher or coach, must know how to specifically define the problem areas that need to be addressed.

Think of it this way. If you're scoring badly, you might start looking at these elements of golf:

- grip
- stance
- swing
- golf course difficulty
- conditions

With more knowledge of the mental game, you also might look at some of these factors:

22

- expectations
- perceptions
- perspective
- personality
- decision making

Have you ever thought of the mental game this way? If your swing has gone sour would you think to look at your grip and maybe your expectations of your swing? There are *mental* fundamentals, as identifiable and specific as the golf grip, that you can learn and master.

If you can do this stretch of conceptualizing the mental components in the same way as you would the physical, let me ask you: Do you know your expectations as well as your grip? Do you know your perspective as well as your swing? If you look at the mental basics this way, you get a clearer idea of how important mental self-awareness is. Few of us practice our perspective as much as we do our swing. In fact, picture the reaction of your friends as you're describing at the 19th hole how a change in your perspective helped you save a par during the round. I assume that you would be hard pressed to explain how perspective or any of the mental elements currently affect your game.

Let's wade straight into this unknown territory. The next chapter will present the brain and how it works. The chapter following that will explain the mind and the mental elements of perception, perspective, anticipation (expectation), intelligence and personality.

THE BRAIN

ince I want you to be able to create your own mental game, a brief excursion into brain physiology is necessary. It is important for you to understand how billions of brain cells make up thousands of "minibrains," which in turn combine into the three "brains" controlling your golf game. Since your conscious mind is only a small part of your brain, it has a hard time controlling everything so that you can focus on making a good golf swing. It's like trying to manage sixty-three invisible Great Danes all struggling to go in different directions. On our journey of understanding you will learn about the brain being like "cookie dough" and how the brain will lie to you. As we go through these two chapters, the "brain" refers to the physical brain, that is, brain cells and their con-

24

nections, while the "mind," more fully described in the next chapter, refers to your thoughts and emotions.

BRAIN CELLS

The brain is made up of billions of individual nerve cells all connected to others, sometimes hundreds or thousands of others, in a system that looks like intertwined tree branches. For the brain to work, each individual cell must "communicate" with the other cells it's connected to. There are chemicals, called neurotransmitters, that enter and exit the cells, enabling the cells to send and receive messages.

The brain works very much like a computer when it processes information. If a switch is off, one thing happens; if on, another. A series of billions of these off/on connections tells the entire collection of brain cells what to do. (The on/off concept is not exactly true, but it's close enough for our purposes.)

This is the brain as a biochemical system, which is much too detailed for us to investigate here. I would like you to keep in mind, though, that the brain, as a biochemical system, relies on the right chemicals in the correct proportions to work efficiently. Your personal habits are important in order for the body to produce the chemicals it needs. A good night's sleep, healthy diet and moderate alcohol consumption are important ingredients to a strong mental game. You can only be as good as your brain chemistry allows. I don't want to preach, but the reality is that playing the mental game with poor neurochemistry is like hitting the ball with dirty clubs.

"MINIBRAINS"

Long before golf existed and before Descartes' philosophy separated the mind from the body, back in the fifth century B.C., Hippocrates decided one day that the brain was the organ of intellect while the heart was the site of the senses. This was one of the first

25

efforts at trying to determine the difference between what the mind did and what the body did. As time marched on, researchers began to recognize that thinking was not just one act that could be localized in a single organ inside the skull. Is balancing the checkbook the same as reading a newspaper or steering a ship?

Franz Joseph Gall in the nineteenth century was one of the first to define the discrete functional parts of the brain, discovering that each mental ability is dependent on a specific group of brain cells. This means that the brain is divided into thousands of "minibrains," each responsible for a specific task. For example there is a minibrain to control the movement of your right thumb, and a different minibrain to control your left index finger. Keep in mind for a moment two things: Each movement (and thought) is controlled by a different minibrain *and* the golf swing is composed of many different areas of the body moving in different ways and with many different thoughts, all occurring at the same time. There is considerable trouble for the golfer in how these physical and mental functions combine with one another.

On a larger scale than these "minibrains" is the concept of hemispheric lateralization. This means that the brain's two hemispheres, the left and right, have different functions.

The left hemisphere is predominantly concerned with speech, while the right is not. This is the reason the left hemisphere is considered dominant. The right side is more global, more feeling, or holistic, not as involved with measurement and concrete details as the left. Many books and articles on the mental game focus on this verbal/feeling division to help the player conceptualize the thought process in golf.

One must use measurement and logic (a left-hemisphere trait) to solve golf's practical problems such as distance to the green and wind direction. The more holistic (right hemisphere) orientation must be used in order to feel the shot and allow the body to swing freely in spite of the dangers of water hazards and out-of-bounds. The idea is to use each hemisphere when it is appropriate to do so and to know when you are analyzing too much or at the wrong time. This is an attractive concept in its simplicity and ease of application to golf. I wish it were this simple. Hold on to your hat; we're going to jump head first into your millions upon millions of brain cells.

26

THE BRAIN AS A UNIT

In order to play golf, or do anything for that matter, you would hope that the brain takes in information and processes the information in a logical manner so we can efficiently go about our business. If it did, this book would be unnecessary and golf would not be the challenge it is. As a matter of fact, we do not perceive information in a logical manner. Nor do we process information as separate and equal bits of data. The brain works logically, yes, but not as you might imagine. Most golfers have seen the hole drastically shrink after watching their opponent's forty-foot putt fall into the hole, leaving the match teetering on their own three-footer. Left-brain logic goes out the window when the emotions get involved.

Forget that the brain operates like a computer and that one hemisphere can do something that the other can't. Instead, think that the brain is like soft cookie dough and like a television news videotape. Think of it like a group of people all talking at once; assume that your brain can be like a bad telephone connection and finally, that your brain can also sort out information in a very controllable step-by-step process. Begin to make new assumptions about how your brain actually works and you will be able to manage what it does on the course a lot better.

Your brain is a wonderful organ and handy to have around. Yet, on its own, it can cause all sorts of problems. The brain can get tired. You can have brain "cramps." It can be like your best friend telling you that things will be all right when they may not be. Or, it can even be like your worst enemy; your brain can lie to you. What you learn in this section will enable you to know what is working in your thought process and what is not.

COOKIE-DOUGH BRAIN

Infants and very young children have brains as impressionable as cookie dough. These brains are directly affected by sights and sounds. Reactions are simple, based upon external stimuli either pleasant or unpleasant, or internal stimuli, such as feeling hungry or cold. Basic drives are strong, for food and for comfort. There is not a lot of thinking. Mostly what the cookie dough brain does is monitor how the child is feeling and observe the world. There's no effort to understand things or make sense of them. This brain never fully grows up. Your awe inspiring first view of Augusta National as you drive down Magnolia Lane is a direct impression, a reaction of the cookie-dough brain. Sometimes such an impression is so strong that it distracts and disrupts normal brain functioning. The cookie-dough brain cannot play good golf. This is what happened to our amateur John at the Masters. Many athletes try to remind their cookie-dough brain that their opponent puts his pants on one leg at a time too or that the situation really isn't that big a deal. Usually negative cookie dough impressions are short lived and easily respond to positive experiences. The majority of mental problems arise when the brain decides to think.

TELEVISION/VIDEOTAPE BRAIN

A phenomenal change occurs in the brain when the growing child learns about words. The significance of the change is that the brain no longer reacts directly to the real world, but rather to what are called mediated impressions. This is the television videotape brain. Pavlov (of the famous dogs) suggested that language introduces changes in the physical makeup of the brain. This means that the words in our heads actually determine how we think and what decisions we can make.

Once our brain has words, it can no longer simply react to the environment. Instead, using the words available to us and those particular ones we choose, everything is reported, just as a news reporter summarizes his or her impressions of an event. We no longer get the real thing, only our unique, individualized, personal news report.

> **What we see and what we think is altered by what we want to see and what we already know.**

That is, your eyes can see the beauty of Augusta while at the same time your verbal brain also "sees" its storied history. This concept is critical to understanding how the mental game works in golf.

28

Our TV brain makes assumptions in deciding what to film, how to write the story and how to edit. The result is that our mental reactions are attuned to what we have already learned, not so much what is actual reality. This is how the brain can lie.

This happens in tournaments sometimes. A player arrives at a new site that has a reputation for unfairness or extreme difficulty. His scores are higher than normal because he is too cautious, playing the course's reputation (the verbal course in his mind) instead of the one in front of his eyes. It is not until someone else gets hot and he realizes the golf course is not some monster that he allows himself to attack it appropriately. The same thing happens if a player watches someone in front of him hit the ball out of bounds or into a water hazard. Immediately the hole is defined in a different way.

So the first conclusion about your own brain that I would like you to make is:

> **The brain does not "see" reality, but has a biased view of the situation that is not always in our own best interest.**

Our cookie-dough brain and our videotape brain can combine to make us feel out of place or inadequate. They can also make us think we are better than we are and get us in over our heads.

TALKING-ALL-AT-ONCE BRAIN

Another aspect the physical brain has is when the minibrains all talk at once. Paul Broca, in the 1860s, felt that the minibrain concept was the best way to understand how the whole brain worked. This is somewhat like the idea that a circus exists as a whole, but the important stuff happens in the separate rings—the clowns throwing pies at each other in the left ring, lions roaring in the right, and the trapeze flying high in the center.

A few years later the English neurologist Hughlings Jackson conjectured that the brain was organized in a "vertical" fashion from the spinal cord through the brain stem to the higher levels, all levels being involved in each mental function. This means that each connected minibrain, each local region of function, from small collections of cells all the way to the two hemispheres, can be involved in a task, a decision or a perception. For example, when you play a hole that you have bogied before, part of your brain is remembering the bogey before and during your swing. (It also means that if you have successfully played a course many times, you will tend to relax and play well again.)

This idea is similar to the golf swing's being defined as a collection of different moves, each one being important, but together creating something greater. One small change in the golf swing, like moving the hips too fast, can throw off the whole thing. It's the same for how the brain works. One small extra thought can ruin everything.

This allows us to draw a second and extremely important conclusion, which is:

[
**Anything that we see or decide to do is
the result of a vast combination of mental
factors, each of which affects what we see and
do in its own way.**
]

In more practical terms this means that the right hemisphere as well as the left is involved in determining distance to the green, that the emotions take part in choosing a club no matter how scientifically the distance is measured and that our left (verbal) brain is always active while we swing at the ball. This is the talking-all-at-once brain.

As the brain develops, it creates easier ways to do its job. That is, the way the brain solves a problem at an early stage in its development is not the way it would do so with more experience. Habits can be established by the brain's constructing neurological shortcuts, by establishing different connections, so that all of the usual brain centers do not have to be employed to complete a task.

A beginning automobile driver, for example, notices everything and can become easily confused by all of the new information entering the brain. Yet within a few months, that same individual can listen to the radio, chew gum and converse with others while holding onto the wheel with one hand and daydreaming about next Saturday's date. The brain has learned what to pay attention to and

30

what can be ignored. Later you will learn how an effective preshot routine can become less so because such a well-ingrained habit can allow the mind to wander too much.

Tension or distraction increases the number of brain areas involved; habit reduces the number. This is a very important concept to know.

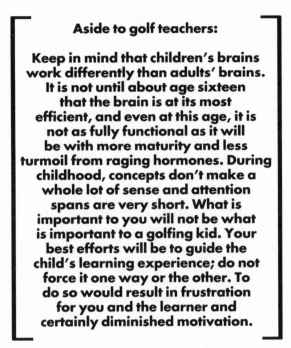

Aside to golf teachers:

Keep in mind that children's brains work differently than adults' brains. It is not until about age sixteen that the brain is at its most efficient, and even at this age, it is not as fully functional as it will be with more maturity and less turmoil from raging hormones. During childhood, concepts don't make a whole lot of sense and attention spans are very short. What is important to you will not be what is important to a golfing kid. Your best efforts will be to guide the child's learning experience; do not force it one way or the other. To do so would result in frustration for you and the learner and certainly diminished motivation.

BAD-CONNECTION BRAIN

With aging, with fatigue, injury or misuse (e.g. alcohol and drugs), brain connections diminish, resulting in less control over actions and reactions. Thoughts are not as clear, problem-solving is not as quick and memory is not as accessible. In a sense, functioning is not lost so much as it becomes disorganized. Learning and stress also add wear and tear to the brain. Even though experience creates more efficient brain functioning, it can add too many thoughts, thereby making an event more complicated than it needs to be. For example, poor putting for a fair number of experienced golfers may be partly the result of diminished neural connections, but it is also the result of these golfers' having learned all the ways a putt can be

31

missed. This is like a bad-telephone-connection brain in that sometimes it works well or too well, other times not so good, and you're never quite sure what you will get, or when.

So we have a third conclusion:

[
The mature brain is both an asset for efficient functioning and a liability in its excess of information or diminished control.
]

LOGICAL BRAIN

Your brain, not always with your awareness, identifies and solves problems a zillion times a day. From choosing a breakfast cereal to turning left in your car to changing the television station to buying a new house, your brain follows a sequence of steps to make every decision. The actual biological process is not well understood as yet, but I want to present a system that is used in countless ways and will pay great dividends when applied to golf. This system was taught by Dr. Roger Kaufman, a graduate school professor of mine. He said that these six steps can be applied to any problem. I agree with him and I think that they are especially useful in golf. The most important of these steps is goal-setting, which we will talk about at length later.

Assume that these six steps are how your brain approaches everything, all the time.

THE BRAIN AT WORK AND PLAY

1. Defines the problem
2. Defines the goal
3. Lists obstacles that interfere with reaching the goal
4. Lists solutions
5. Implements the best solution
6. Evaluates and improves

Later, we're going to take a look at golfer Jim's thought process before he hit his tee shot. Before we do that, let's apply the six-step process to a more critical situation so you will have a good idea of how it works. Take, for instance, a car accident. In a crisis situation our minds work very hard indeed. Let's put Jim's mind into a potential accident to see the thinking process unfold in ultraslow-motion.

Thanks to us, Jim's mind and body are now driving down a multi-lane highway toward the golf course in the family sedan, listening to the radio, not a care in the world. There are cars at either side of him, and in front, about a thirty yards or so, is an old pickup truck piled high with empty steel oil drums held together with a single, thin, fraying hemp rope. All of a sudden, the rope breaks and an oil drum falls upright in Jim's lane. What does his mind do? Most people say "slam on the brakes" or "panic," but this is not what happens.

The first thing Jim's mind does is say to itself, "Gee. There's a steel oil drum in my lane." That is all: a simple, efficient notice of a change in his situation. What do you think Jim's mind would have done if a little clod of dirt had fallen off the truck instead of an oil drum? He would have noticed the dirt, then promptly forgotten it. A change in the situation is noticed, but is not defined as something that requires any action.

However, in the case of a steel oil drum, the mind first notices the event, then catalogues it as a problem requiring Jim's attention. So the first thing Jim's mind does is to notice what is happening and then defines it as a problem: "There is a steel oil drum in my lane and I've got a problem."

Problem: Steel oil drum in lane

Next, and this is critically important, Jim defines his goal, in this case to avoid smashing into the oil drum.

Goal: Avoid an accident

Remember this point: **We humans are always goal oriented, sometimes without being consciously aware of the goal.**

After defining his goal, Jim then lists all the things he can

33

think of that might stop him from reaching it. The cars on either side may be a problem. The time to impact at his speed is 1.7 seconds. The brakes have been acting funny lately and he meant to have them fixed. He notes anything he can think of that might have to be included in his problem solving. This is his list of obstacles:

Obstacles:

1. Other cars
2. Time to impact
3. Tension
4. Etc.

Next, he lists

Solutions:

1. Brake
2. Panic
3. Jump in the back seat
4. Swerve to the side
5. Pretend it is all a dream
6. Etc.

The fourth step is simply a creative listing of possible solutions with no evaluation, criticism or judgment. Next, he will choose and implement the best solution.

During this step, he would compare how each possible solution would work to reach his goal while overcoming any obstacles that he had listed. For example, swerving to one side, solution number four, could not be used because he would hit one of the cars driving alongside. So, step three is listing obstacles, step four is listing solutions and step five is picking the best one. In Jim's case he chose and applied solution number one.

Pick best solution: Brake

The last step the mind takes is to evaluate the results and change whatever needs to be changed. Jim immediately evaluated the results and realized that the brakes weren't working well enough to stop him in time.

Revise: Accident still possible

He then went through the entire process again. Same problem, same goal, but the car on his left has continued on, so an original hurdle has been removed and solution number four can be used too. Jim has slammed on his brakes and swerved to the left to avoid the oil drum—all in less than the time it takes to swing a golf club (which Jim will do for us a little later).

For our purposes, this is how your brain approaches and solves every golf problem that it encounters. The brain always has a goal, conscious or not, that it seeks to reach. If you recall, the golfer Nick, who missed a short putt playing in the PGA, actually reached his goal. His brain had at least two goals, first to make a good score, a birdie in this case. And when that didn't happen, he set a second goal, to discharge his frustration, which he accomplished by backhanding the putt. I'll say it again later, but remember, golfers always have two sets of goals, one having to do with golf, the other involving the emotions.

$$\left[\begin{array}{c} \textbf{The emotional goal is always more important} \\ \textbf{to the brain than the golf goal.} \end{array} \right]$$

BIORHYTHMS

We have not talked about biorhythms or cycles, yet these are important components of the physical brain too. There are a couple of obvious cycles that affect brain functioning. The sleep/wake cycle is common to everyone. We all know how poorly our brains work when we are overly tired, sleepy or jet-lagged. Women are aware of the impact of their monthly menstrual cycle. For some, the premenstrual phase is a time of irritation, poor concentration, lessened judgment and a host of other debilitating symptoms.

35

Some biorhythms are short, just minutes in duration, while some are much longer. It is not known how important these are in mental functioning overall or for short periods of time. For this reason we will not discuss them. There is some suggestion from research that your ability to concentrate can cycle up and down in a period much shorter than the average length of a golf match. Maybe this is one reason why strings of bad holes can occur so often. There may be other cycles that last weeks, months or even longer. Once this is understood, players may be able to monitor their cycles and compensate for this normal ebb and flow of brain capacity.

PLAYING THE MENTAL SYMPHONY

All the minibrains, talking at once, must be unified to produce a controlled, smooth, effective, repeating golf swing. You probably are now aware that this is not easily done. The best we can do is to increase the chances that all the minibrains are talking about the same thing and have relatively similar goals. French critic M. Auguste Bailly helpfully suggests that the mind can be compared to a symphony and that each of our minds can be seen as chords comprising harmony rather than a Tower of Babble. We are after this harmony.

THE MINIBRAINS BECOME THREE BRAINS

It is impossible to describe here all the kinds and locations of our symphony of brain functions and, in fact, they are not all known or understood. For our purposes, there are three symphonic sections (or three brains we will talk a lot about later). Think of them, perhaps, as the strings, horns and percussion section of a symphony orchestra, or maybe the lead vocalist, guitar and drums of a rock band.

The most basic section of the brain has to do with physical movement. A collection of our minibrains must be involved in our physical acts, that is, causing the action and being aware of the

36

action as it takes place. This is not as much under your control as you might imagine. Touching a hot stove and reflexively pulling your hand back, for instance, involves only your spinal cord and not your brain.

A portion of this brain is what Pavlov termed an "integrative reflex," which is a series of unconscious movements. This is what happens when you are attacked by a wasp on the tee and are able to swat at it while ducking and keeping your balance. You fight off the wasp while the rest of your mind makes sure you don't fall. You are not conscious of your brain's doing the work to keep you upright. (Lifting the head during the swing is most likely a Pavlovian integrative reflex, too, and is thus difficult to change.) It might make you feel better sometimes if you give yourself the benefit of the doubt on some of your mishits. Trying to swing a smooth long-iron might be affected in ways beyond your conscious control.

The second section of our brain symphony is our emotions and drives: sexual, aggressive, self-preserving, etc. Our drives are very powerful determinants of our behavior. Lower forms of animals have their entire lives determined by instincts and drives. We have much more freedom to make choices, but only if the drives are under control. Players who make the mistake of playing angry golf are expressing drives rather than hitting a good golf shot.

Emotions are best understood as a combination of our drives and our mind's perception of a situation. For example, if you expect to hit a good tee shot and don't, your frustration is the result of your mental definition of the situation and your drive to succeed. If you had no expectations for the shot, the results would not cause any emotional response.

The third section of our mental symphony is our thoughts, which we will cover in detail in the next chapter. **All** three sections outlined above are involved in **all** of our activities. Thus, our mental symphony or rock band is made up of our doing brain, our emotional/sensing brain and our thinking brain, each being made up of countless minibrains.

FINALLY

At this point I hope you clearly understand the idea that the brain is not like a computer—good information in, good information out.

37

Instead, the brain, by its nature, twists things around for its own needs. Reality is only a starting point. What you see from the tee is unique. What combination of minibrains you use to play your shot is not the same as anyone else's. What you must do to manage your minibrains is personal to you. It is like practice. Some players need a lot, some very little. There is no one right method of improving your swing. Likewise, there is no one method to line up your minibrains like ducks in a row. Next, I want you to learn about your mind, that part of you that only you can experience and control (or so we like to think).

THE MIND

he brain is the mind's connection to the body. For the body to drive a car, write a poem or swing a golf club, the mind must be involved in some way. Our efforts in this section will be to understand what the mind is, how it operates and how to use it to play your best golf.

Part of the concept of mind is that it is the portion of the brain that gives us self-awareness. Lower animals have brains that enable them to adjust to their changing environment, avoid danger and procreate their species. The difference between their brains and ours, what creates our human "mind," is the degree of self-awareness we have *and* our self-talk. Our minds can take us into the past and future, to events here on earth and everywhere in the universe as well as communicate with others now and later. Right now, you can think about the last time you played your favorite course, the last time you hit out of bounds, the last time you played fantastic golf. You can imagine playing the Old Course at St Andrews or the newest layout in Florida. Your mind can take you anywhere you can imagine, from dining with a movie star in the south of France, to walking naked down Main Street or sinking up to your neck in a sand trap.

We humans have a marvelously complicated mind, especially when compared to other animals. It is hard to imagine, for instance, a dog looking in the mirror and wondering about getting gray hair. Both self-observation and anticipation of the future are nonexistent or severely limited in lower animals. But in humans, anticipation of the future is so strong that it can distract us from the task at hand. Many tournaments have been lost down the stretch by the player who is too busy preparing his acceptance speech to hit any more good golf shots.

Our higher mental processes (as opposed to reflexes, balance and the like), arise out of our verbal communication with others. With words we can represent important information. If I say "cold," you know what that means without having to currently experience it yourself. You can easily see how this applies to golf if your mind thinks of the word "shank" before a tough pitch shot. It is a common ploy of gamesmanship to casually point out a hazard to the opponent. What this does is to create an emphasis on the hazard in the player's mind using this effect of verbal reality.

Do you remember my asking you if you practiced perspective as much as your swing? In this section we will investigate some of the more important elements of the mind. These are some of the reasons why we need to do so:

- The mind makes things up.
- The mind pretends to know the future.
- The mind gets scared of ghosts.
- The mind remembers too much and often the wrong thing.
- The mind measures with a ruler that is always changing.
- The mind makes mistakes.

This chapter presents some of the ways your mind works and some of the elements of the mental game. If you think of your brain

40

as computer hardware, the mind is the software. When you use mental techniques, the elements described in this chapter are what you are training to work for you.

PERCEPTION

The perceiving mind, remember, does not perceive reality. The mind can "see" only an edited version of the world—and can make mistakes. Psychologist Daniel Gilbert compared the operation of the mind to a library cataloging system. He said that the brain files information as either true or false, like a library would catalogue books as either fiction or nonfiction. For cataloging books in a library, one simple method is to put a colored dot on the spines of fiction books and no dot on nonfiction books. As long as all books were read and catalogued before being put on the shelf, this system would work very well. The flaw in the system is that if a book is put on the shelf without being catalogued, it would have no dot and you would assume that it was nonfiction. Only later, after you arrived home and opened it up, would you learn the truth.

So a flaw in the way the mind works is that something the mind perceives as true is treated as truth until proven false.

In golf, if one of our minibrains thinks something, like "Uh-oh, I may hook this one," just before the downswing, our mind believes this thought to be true. It cannot delay making a decision until all information is collected. This is like assuming that an unmarked book in the library is nonfiction without taking the time to open it up and take a look. Therefore, one of the primary "mental game" problems for the golfer is that perception of what is real is based on assumptions that may not be true.

Another example of this effect is when players feel out of their league, no matter if it's on the tour or a Tuesday-night-after-work nine holes. A feeling of belonging is necessary for you to play your normal game. If your mind has made the assumption that you are over your head, it will believe that for a long time until something symbolic, like a victory or a high enough finish, adds the right kind of new information to the brain. Most tour rookies have this feeling of not yet belonging. Defeating a parent for the first time is also a perception problem of fiction being stronger than truth. Most kids

41

have the skill to beat Mom or Dad long before they actually accomplish the feat.

MENTAL SYSTEM FAILURE

Our minds are a series of minibrains or information-processing units. Simply put, one minibrain might measure the distance of a putt, another its importance. Each small bit of everything we think, feel and do is put through its own series of processes, and information is passed from one minibrain to another until a unified whole perspective or action is created. If any one of the processing units is defective, the entire network fails to function correctly.

When such a collection of systems is malfunctioning, the tendency is for a reaction or thought to be incomplete. That is, the mind stops working on a thought too early and makes specific kinds of errors. The errors are that ideas or feelings are defined as true when they may not be, like the fiction and nonfiction library books, and that:

> [**There is a tendency to trust what we believe we know, in spite of new information to the contrary.**]

Imagine a tour player about to hit his approach shot to the 18th green. Birdie is needed for the win. If his brain were simply receiving and processing information, he would note the distance and other factors like wind direction and smoothly hit an 8-iron. In this situation, though, he is under considerable mental stress because he has never won a tournament before. In the one chance to win he had a year ago, he choked on his approach to the last hole and hooked his ball into the water hazard.

To make this simple, his perceiving mind is focused on two things: gathering information by which to choose the right club and his fast-growing seeds of nervousness, both equally real to the mind that is trying to keep things in perspective. In addition, his mind is also creating something to think about that has nothing to do with hitting the ball. "This is the most important shot of your life!" it says. Since his mind is under stress, even though self-created, it begins to break down and information is not fully processed. That bad shot of a year ago gets a little too much attention and his thought process

42

doesn't move forward much. The feeling of "choke" arises. One of his minibrains believes that he will choke. Another one, controlling movement, intercepts this idea in midswing and, in attempting to prevent the hook that caused disaster last year, causes him to push the ball into the right side-bunker just short of the green. The mind attempts to coordinate all of the minibrains no matter how opposite the information might be. (The weird happenings in dreams is caused by this phenomenon.) This unfortunately is normal, common and, while awake and trying to play golf, detrimental to playing our best.

PERSPECTIVE

The mind that creates perspective also creates problems. Perspective is how we define what we see. In an ideal situation, what we see and how we put it into perspective would be the same. This is like saying that all three-foot uphill putts are essentially the same, no matter if you are playing for a two- dollar nassau or for the National Open. We know that this is not true. Physically, yes, a three-foot putt is always a three-foot putt. But mentally, they can be worlds apart. The difference is perspective.

I'm sure you can recall when you first hit a shot that until then had been impossible, like carrying a pond for the first time. When you accomplished it, your perception of the shot changed. Perspective can be positive, that difficult situations are challenges, not problems. It can be negative too; a particular course, for example, is defined as too hard or not made for your game. What perspective can be is that no shot is impossible; you just haven't done it yet. Using perspective to your advantage is one of the important elements of the mental game.

VALUES

Part of the reason why our perspective mind causes distress is that our minds constantly value and judge things. We respond to situations depending, in part, on what we think is important. The mind is always measuring outcomes and comparing results. In golf it is often evaluating such things as high earnings, Major victories, a low handicap or good distance off the tee.

The golfer who yells at himself for being the dumbest thing on two feet when he misses a putt is responding to a value system. This is not to say that missing putts should be taken lightly, but we should create a value system that promotes self-esteem and good play, not one that criticizes and demeans. What we value and how we value it can cause anxiety, depression or anger, none of which is helpful in producing our best performance. What happens is that the valuing mind focuses more on personal and cultural values than on golf performance. I can remember hitting a very good tee shot on one hole while out playing with three young professionals. My shot was followed by three screaming tee shots at least twenty yards longer than mine. Did I feel good about my shot? Heck no. Once the other "guys" (one of them a lady) hit farther, my valuing mind threw out the personal yardstick and evaluated my shot by comparing it to the others'. I came in last. For the next few holes I tried harder to outhit them, my swing fell apart and I played lousy golf. This lesson I learned will be important to remember when we talk about aggressive golf being stupid golf.

MEMORY

The mind that remembers is certainly an asset. Many books on the mental game present techniques of recalling your best day or your best shot in order to get into the correct mental state to play to your maximum ability. The player is encouraged to recall in detail, using all of his senses, the perfect shot. This seems to focus the mind, clear away doubts and remind the player that now is no different from before when success was achieved. For the most part, this technique is very effective. The only fly in the ointment is that nagging memories of negative experiences seem to have equal, if not stronger, power.

Much of our perspective is based on well-entrenched or intense memories, not so much on recent experience or what we hope to achieve. To play your best, you must take into account your perspective, of the shot and of your ability to play the shot, not pretending anything is good when your perspective says otherwise. If you take perspective into account, it can be changed for the better using mental game techniques.

44

ANTICIPATION

The anticipating mind predicts the future. Unfortunately, if a future event is important, the mind can worry about it. But worry is like building a bridge before you get to the river. Instead of waiting for reality, the anticipating mind is trying to decide what kind of bridge to build before seeing how wide the river is. You have undoubtedly had the experience of worrying about what club you're going to use on a hole that you haven't arrived at yet. That is the anticipating mind at work. Identifying the problem correctly and putting the mind to work on the problem at hand is part of the task of the mental game.

Since the mind usually assumes things to be true, the good thing about the anticipating mind (if you have been successful before) is that it will assume success. The down side is that if you haven't been a winner or if you've been having bad luck, it will assume that failure should be expected (or that your bad luck will continue), and preparations for failure should be made. If your mind is preparing for failure, it cannot be preparing for success.

The mind, therefore, creates self-fulfilling prophesies. Whatever we expect, we will unconsciously try to make happen, even if that means losing or playing poorly. Logically, this doesn't seem to make sense. Why set ourselves up to fail when winning is so enjoyable?

We do it, logically enough, to avoid anxiety.

The mind likes things to be simple and predictable. What we unconsciously believe to be true must be true or we become anxious about our belief system. Anxiety is an emotion that tells us something is terribly wrong. (Anxiety is what causes neurosis and is the foundation of such severe psychopathology as multiple personality disorders and hysterical paralysis.) So whatever causes anxiety, even if it is something not true, the mind tries to make true. Fear of success and fear of failure are both driven by this anxiety. When we are outside our comfort zone (to be discussed later) we often do whatever it takes to get back in. Anxiety also causes us to "miss it quick." If a shot, especially a putt, feels too difficult, we swing quickly to get it over with and reduce the anxiety. Disappointment is easier to handle than anxiety.

It gets worse. If the mind were alone in producing anticipation, you would think that mind control techniques would work

45

fairly well. The physical brain, however, also gets into the act. Some interesting physiological experiments show us what happens. Since the brain is divided into minibrains, experimenters can measure how involved a particular minibrain is in various situations. For example, if you are raising your right hand, the area in your left hemisphere that controls that movement can be detected by measuring an increase of blood flow or glucose use in that area.

In a mind-body experiment, researcher Roland asked a subject to pay attention to her finger because it was going to be lightly touched. It was never touched, but numerous areas of the brain associated with that finger had an increase in blood flow. By anticipating the touch, this subject was able to create a new reality in her brain. We do this all the time. A common example is a phobia. For some people, entering an elevator or flying in a plane is impossible because their minds have created the reality that this experience is life threatening. The body then panics.

For those of you without a phobia, there are a couple of other common examples of how the mind can create powerful responses. Have you ever had a dream where you felt you were falling? The brain can make that experience so real you actually feel like you are plummeting fifty stories, waking with a start just before you hit. Or, have you ever gone to bed at night, aware you had to wake up especially early and you woke up a minute or two before the alarm went off? Who woke you up? Your unconscious mind did. The mind is an awesomely powerful creator of reality, both now and in anticipating the future. It is easy to see that if the mind can create reality in a dream, it certainly has a lot of involvement in our fears and uncertainties on the golf course.

INTELLIGENCE

One of my favorite statements about golf is that anyone foolish enough to play the game is not wise enough to play it well. Actually, a common problem is that most of us are too smart too often for our own good. Too much analysis, as you know, causes paralysis and a host of other problems.

Intelligence must be applied in the correct way to insure good play. But what is intelligence, and how is it applied? Psychology has divided up "intelligence" into many parts, such as understanding

46

words, predicting sequences of events or doing arithmetic problems. Each of us has different levels of the many subdivisions of intelligence. The best summation I know of for general intelligence is that it is "awareness." The intelligent golfer must have an awareness of:

1. temperament
2. expectations
3. tendencies
4. abilities
5. strengths and weaknesses
6. swing characteristics
7. club performance
8. demands of the course
9. ball-flight laws
10. probability theory

This is an incomplete list of course. However, it gives you an idea of some of the different kinds of intelligence involved in golf.

Another way of looking at intelligence is as information-processing. There are three basic human receiving channels: auditory, visual and kinesthetic, or in other words, hearing, seeing and doing. We each have a different "intelligence" for each channel. It is the rare and gifted person who is equally good in each way. All of them are required in the play of good golf.

The verbally aware or the auditory learner is usually described by others as "smart." These people, who are usually the "A" students in school, are good thinkers and analyzers and probably have what is called "a good left brain." Obviously, golf requires a fair amount of thinking about the requirements of a shot or one's position in the field. The current reliance on yardage markers is a verbal-awareness characteristic. Some players need this kind of information more than others, depending on how their brains work.

Almost opposite to the verbal learner is the person who is visually aware. This person can "sense" things well without thoughtful analysis. Without measuring specifics, the visually gifted can know what needs to be known and done. Many people cannot trust this

47

sense because it is not easily measured or it is somehow not real enough. Seeing the line of a putt or "knowing" the shot is a 7-iron no matter what the distance is due (in part) to this kind of awareness.

Similar to visual intelligence is the kinesthetic sense. This body sense is the least thoughtful and the most automatic of our intelligence. We all know of people with exceptional coordination who could do it all, like Michael Jordan, Babe Ruth and Pélé. When asked how they manage their amazing deeds, they would reply, "I don't know, I just do it." This seems to minimize the "intelligent" aspect of this awareness because it isn't thoughtful; but it is still an awareness, still high in some and low in others and still important in golf. The kinesthetic intelligence comes into play when you try to "feel" a chip shot before you hit it. No matter what your level in each of these types of awareness, you can improve your ability in all of them and compensate for your limitations when you reach your ceiling.

> **For readers who are teachers, this concept of verbal, visual and kinesthetic learning is important to remember in deciding how to approach each student. The verbal learner, for example, will be most comfortable in discussing concepts first before trying them out. The opposite is true of the kinesthetic learner, who would much rather feel the swing you want him to learn. Showing the visual learner what to do is easy and very effective. Use examples, mirrors or videotape. Utilize all channels for the best effect, but emphasize the one that works best for each student.**

PERSONALITY

Next in our exploration of the golfer's mind is personality. Personality is the total of *individual* traits, behaviors and attitudes that make a person unique. It includes such characteristics as assertiveness, toughness, stability, rigidity, composure and self-suf-ficiency. It also includes our sense of self, our definition of who we are. As a golfer, you know how self-esteem can get battered on the course. Isn't it interesting that we take our egos out to play knowing we are risking stepping on them with size-ten spikes?

48

Our ego, that self-aware part of us that copes with bogeys as well as birdies, is called upon with every shot, with every decision, with every result, good or bad. Golf is not simply a game. It is a constant struggle to overcome obstacles and cope with numerous mistakes. To borrow a bit from Samuel Johnson, golf is a game that demonstrates the triumph of hope over experience. The professional golfer must put his ego on the line each week, fully aware that his chances of winning are, at best, less than one in ten. The weekend player anticipates a fun day in spite of expecting fifty or sixty bad shots.

This can be done because of ego defense mechanisms. These psychological entities are created in the mind to protect the ego from harm. "Sour grapes" is a common reaction when the golfer cannot get what he wanted: "I didn't really try hard," or "I don't really want it," or "I don't care," etc. These defenses protect us so we will want to go out another day, or they restrict how hard we try so we don't get too badly shaken by the results. Our personalities are both an asset and a liability for good golf; so are our efforts to preserve our dignity and self- esteem.

SUMMARY

For you readers who are interested in knowing more about the mind and brain, there are many books and articles that will further explain their intricate workings. My brief yet somewhat detailed description of the brain and the thought processes of the mind cannot do justice to the complicated events that occur inside your brain millions of times each second. What I want you to keep in your memory is that the mind/brain you use in playing golf is your biggest hurdle if you do not know how to manage it.

You will misperceive situations, you will jump to conclusions, you will overreact, you will make up stories, you will do a host of things not at all related to the playing of golf. You will do this not because your brain is damaged or you are not very bright, but because this is how the mind works. Mainly, your mind will unconsciously do whatever it takes to avoid feeling bad, anxious, out of control or stupid. In spite of this, your mind is your staunchest ally if you learn how it works and how to direct it.

If your mind has perceived and processed this material on the brain and mind, you have become much better equipped to understand the human being who plays golf. I cannot stress enough the importance of knowing these basics, especially since they are very abstract and probably something you have not thought about before.

I want you to remember that the mental game is as individualized as the physical game, vastly more complicated and easily oversimplified. Remember too, that mental components cannot be simply selected or changed like a 6-iron for a 7 when the wind shifts. This is like Don the pro telling Judi to relax or John the amateur pretending to be playing just another tournament during the Masters. Just because you say it or want it to happen does not make it so. The mind responds to what it believes, not to what you tell it. In order to play your best, and teach well, you must realize that you have to be able to trust every club in your mental bag. And, of course, you can never be sure you are correct in the mental game because it is so difficult to monitor and measure.

The next chapter builds upon what you now know about how the mind and brain work. It will generalize concepts even though each of us is unique. As we go along, always apply your own experience to the ideas so they make good sense to you, and always assume that anyone else's experience is different and equally correct, especially if you teach golf.

THE MIND
OF THE
GOLFER

Sometimes I think the Scots only invented the game as a good excuse to drink their native whiskey. After a round, sometimes only a splash of Laphroaig can temper the agony of the day's trials. So why do we do it? You may as well ask why we ride roller coasters or watch scary movies or why we attempt a 3-wood over a lake King Kong couldn't carry. You've heard the descriptions of golf, a "good walk spoiled" or an "exercise in futility." I don't know of a game that embraces so completely the human heart and at the same time seizes so violently at the throat.

This chapter will explain how our minds go about figuring out what is happening when we play. We will talk about thought-processing, emotional reactions, defending our pride and a considerable amount more. By the end of this section you will know a great deal about what goes on in two of your minds, the thinking and sensing minds, as you play.

THE FOUR BALL

It's late on a Sunday afternoon and the autumn sun is a hazy orange ball in the darkening sky. The air is becoming crisp as the match arrives at the last tee all square. First to tee up are the winners of the last hole, courtesy of Jim's chip in from short of the green for a sudden and unexpected birdie. Bill and Dennis, the now-tied opponents, are disgruntled and ready to exact their revenge on the short par-5 18th.

"Alright, partner," Brent says to Jim, "do your best."

Most of us have been in a similar situation, needing and wanting to do our best. That is what sports and golf are all about. Let's take a slow stroll through the mind of each golfer prior to his tee shot and investigate what goes on. Jim is a good golfer, at about the same level as his opponent Bill but much less competitive. He has played fairly well today so he expects to hit his driver without any problem. Jim's primary thought is to hit a long ball because his partner Brent hasn't been able to do much yet and is unlikely to get anything going now. Brent, on the other hand, has thoughts enough for the both of them. He desperately wants to beat his neighbor Bill, is disappointed in his inability to help his partner, wants to correct his pull hook and is worried about how long the round has taken because of the dinner party his wife has planned. Brent is focused on creating a quick birdie and rushing home to cope with an irritated spouse.

The friendly opponents are thinking too. Bill, like Brent, is also having a bad day, cursing his bad luck from the very first approach shot. He is wondering what evil lurks for him along this fairway. Dennis, who has the weakest game, is cruising along as always: hacking, slicing and topping. Nothing disturbs his lack of concentration, at least his golf concentration. His mind is all over the place, from analyzing last night's business report to planning tomorrow's lunch. At the moment he is thinking about using a different ball and wondering if he should try one of Bill's with the new dimple pattern for better distance.

Let's first look at Jim since he is on the tee. He is responding to

52

Brent's encouragement to "do his best." His mind begins to define "best." At first, best is in the fairway. Then it becomes long and in the fairway. Then he decides best is long, in the fairway and down the right side. Finally, best is the best he has ever hit on this hole. His mind compares "long tee shot" to his swing ability (possible, but not real likely). His mind recalls his last attempt at a long ball (disastrous) and his last efforts on this hole (he'd rather not talk about it). Jim thinks about how nice it would be to win this hole for his team, how nice to carry his partner one more time, how much luck he has enjoyed so far (has it run out?), and how hard he could swing and still connect for a good one. Muscles in his shoulders and arms begin to tense in anticipation of a violent slash at the ball.

If Jim is like the rest of us, and he is, he will decide to swing hard at the ball, and he will do a poor job of it. He will do a poor job because his mind did not pay attention to his thoughts.

We do funny things with our minds. We ask it to solve a problem and sometimes don't wait for the answer, usually when we need a good answer the most.

JIM'S THOUGHT PROCESS

Since Jim avoided that accident on the way to the course using the six-step problem-solving process, let's analyze his golf thoughts using that same concept. First, what's his problem? To make it incredibly simple, we shall list only five of the problems his mind is trying to solve (you may have thought there was only one):

1. Hitting the ball long
2. Worrying about his partner's game
3. His partner's definition of "best"
4. An increase in muscle tension
5. Recalling the last time he played this hole

For each of these problems Jim's mind has created a goal, whether or not Jim is consciously aware of it.

53

1. A tee shot over the bunker on the right side close enough to reach the green in two

2. His partner to play well enough to win the hole on his own ball

3. A better tee shot than either has ever seen on this hole

4. Get rid of tension quick

5. Don't screw up

An interesting set of goals, don't you think? Can you see that some would help him hit a good tee shot and some would not? Do you think that goal number two might cause some confusion or uncertainty for Jim? Or how about number three? Talk about pressure. Number four might produce a "miss it quick" kind of swing, while number five certainly is proposing negative thinking. Keep in mind that Jim is thinking all of these thoughts and a lot more while standing on the tee preparing to swing.

Each of Jim's goals while on the 18th tee has its own set of hurdles or obstacles. For example, his goal of hitting over the right fairway bunker has at least four:

1. It is a 220-yard carry

2. It is slightly against the wind

3. Jim tends to pull the ball when he swings too hard

4. He is not focused or relaxed enough

However, he does have a number of solutions to choose from in order to reach his goal of a long tee shot:

1. Hit it quick

2. Think; relax, it is only a game

3. Swing as hard as he can

4. Recall the lesson on long driving and do what he learned

5. Use one of those illegal "hot" balls

6. Etc.

Which one he chooses depends on how aware he is of all his options, all of his obstacles and all of his *other* goals. This is not easy in the heat of the moment; recall that pressure produces mental system failure. Poor Jim was not aware of the increased muscle tension in his shoulders and arms, nor was he aware of his goal to get rid of it quickly. In addition, he had no conscious clue to his wish that Brent would be the hero at the last hole. All in all, Jim did what he most wanted to do: swing with his obvious best effort, the maximum violent swing, which left Brent with the task of winning the hole when Jim's ball sailed left out of bounds.

SENSING

Let's now take a look at how the emotions operate. We may as well choose Jim's partner, Brent, since he is next on the tee and has a torrent of anguish coursing through his veins. All of us know about feelings; we have them every day, just like thoughts. Even though our feelings are logical in the sense that they are normal responses to our experiences, they are illogical to the extent they are not controlled by our cerebral cortex (the thinking brain). Our emotions are experienced when we perceive a situation that stimulates them.

When our emotions are stimulated, a series of events take place. Our man Brent, and all the rest of us, have two nervous systems: the peripheral nervous system, which controls the skeletal muscles such as the biceps, and the autonomic nervous system, which controls smooth muscles and glands, and things like heart rate and respiration. One half of the autonomic system is the sympathetic nervous system, which directly controls our physiological arousal. This is the part of us that responds when we are under stress. The other half of the autonomic system is the parasympathetic nervous system, which logically enough, tones down the sympathetic responses to produce a balance between them called "homeostasis." So one part of us gets agitated under stress while the other calms us down as soon as it can. Brent's sympathetic nervous system is getting agitated.

55

FIGHT OR FLIGHT

In a nutshell (no pun intended), this is what is happening in Brent's brain. His mind is thinking about all of the possible bad outcomes and the importance of a good one. He wants very much to win. This combination of drive and his expectations has gotten him worked up. So his thinking brain (cortex) is mulling over how frustrating it will be to lose and his body is tensing up. His sensing brain (limbic system, including his hypothalamus and his reticular activating system) is turning up the biochemical arousal system. The pituitary gland is stimulated and releases a hormone (ACTH) that stimulates the adrenal glands to arouse other areas of the body with adrenaline and noradrenaline. Coupled with an increase in heart rate, respirations and blood pressure, as well as an increase in blood to the muscles, Brent is ready to fight this battle of the 18th hole and dominance over his friend Bill. You probably got the picture that Brent is overreacting, and he is, but at the same time he is reacting normally to his perception of the situation.

This is what the hustler is looking for when he gambles. He tries to set up a wager that puts his victim into a situation that stimulates the limbic system. That tight collar and those sweaty palms are your perceptions and nervous system at work.

You may have heard of it before, but it bears repeating that we all have a primitive biological response to stress that is called the "fight or flight" response. This is our physical response, summarized above, that evolved out of a desire to avoid being lunch for a saber-toothed tiger. Under threat, real or imagined, our bodies become activated in order to fight off an attack or to run from it, hence the "fight" and the "flight." While this response had clear advantages when it came to hungry saber-toothed tigers, it has decided disadvantages when it comes to swinging a golf club or standing over a five-foot downhill putt.

Unfortunately, this fight-or-flight response is pretty easy to get started. You have experienced it from a near miss in your car or from a sudden loud bang behind you. Even during sleep we can awaken in a cold sweat, thanks to an aroused autonomic nervous system that is reacting only to a dream. It is just Brent's mind that is creating his trouble. He is thinking about how he wants to beat Bill and how terrible his game has been today. He is visualizing a bad swing and an equally bad result. He is feeling his tension and is getting angry at himself for getting tense. He also hates the idea that the match got all the way to the 18th hole anyway because now his wife is going to be furious.

Picture this sad scene: Brent, keyed up, has just watched his friend and partner Jim lash at the ball with an uncharacteristic loss of control. As we know, the ball flew out of bounds. Where does this leave Brent? His friend has carried him all day so he can't be angry at the guy. Their fate rests with him. The pressure builds. He hears a muffled chuckle from, he thinks, that moron Bill. "Alright," he says to himself, "this is war." A saber-toothed tiger roars in his subconscious. He, too, lashes at the ball, which booms off the clubface not to return to earth for 230 yards, rocketing, by sheer luck, the entire distance down that ever-so-appealing right center fairway.

"Oh, my gosh," was all Bill could say. The ball was now in his court, so to speak. Bill isn't a moron, Brent's temporary definition notwithstanding. He's a nice guy, but today, one without good fortune. So far, he has suffered four 3-putts, including three lip-outs, one out-of-bounds, one lost ball and two unlucky bounces. His mind on the 18th is a very interesting one, like yours sometimes.

EXPECTATIONS

After Jim's shot, Bill was thinking that lady luck may have just returned after a long absence. Then Brent shocked him with his coming-out-of-his-socks swing, the kind that usually ends up in the parking lot. He quickly reviewed all of the bad luck he has had so far and anticipated all the things that could go wrong on 18. A black cloud was beginning to descend over his heart when he suddenly recalled a formula he read in a golf magazine somewhere:

$$F = E - R$$

"That's it," he thought, "I must manage my frustration so I can have a chance of hitting the ball well enough to pull this match out." Since your library may not be the same as Bill's, I will explain the formula. Frustration is equal to the gap between Expectations and Results. This means that Bill's emotions were being tormented by his expecting good things from his swing, and instead, suffering the fate of the Titanic. The article he read suggested creating high expectations but then quickly accepting whatever the results happened to be. This, the writer proclaimed, was the key to coping with the varied fortunes of golf. Bill realized he hadn't been accepting reality, but had been focusing on the gap between what he wanted and what he got. Concentrating on the difference between what he expected and what he got was fueling his frustration.

Just in time, Bill was able to change his perception, focusing now on accepting the past results and setting up new expectations. This enabled him to alter his perspective on the 18th hole. Instead of dreading another experience of futility, he was able to define the hole as a chance to outthink his bad luck and to maybe just beat these guys. A smooth swing put him into the left fairway bunker, but in a decent lie.

FOCUSING

"Okay. How do we stand?" Dennis wasn't quite sure of the status of the match, although he knew they had lost the 17th. Some people would complain that Dennis had trouble paying attention, but that wasn't true. In fact, he paid great attention to whatever he wanted to and none at all when he didn't want to. Dennis could switch his focus from his stock funds to talking about the weather to his golf swing faster than a concrete fairway. This is what his mind did on the tee once his partner explained the situation:

1. "Wow, the match is all even"
2. He calculated the money and pride to be won or lost
3. He evaluated the demands of the hole
4. He noted the wind direction and speed and the dryness of the fairway
5. He took in how the others players hit
6. He recalled how poorly he was hitting his driver
7. Chose his 3-wood
8. Did his preshot routine

58

9. Noticed some extra tension and relaxed

10. Focused on the ball

Although his physical skills are untutored, Dennis more than makes up for it in mental awareness. His attention followed a useful path from a wide external view of the wager and course conditions to a narrow focus on his internal arousal level. He also did something more astounding, he fell into "the zone."

This doesn't happen often, but Dennis did it. The zone is a mental state that appears to enable the player to do his absolute best. It is achieved when the player has no fear. It is almost thoughtless, effortless, feeling one with the world, completely immersed in the play and in complete control. Dennis accidentally created this state by being very interested in the outcome of the match, so his arousal was high. But at the same time, he focused only on hitting the ball and did not worry about where it went.

He fulfilled the basic conditions for being in the zone: high interest and a nonjudgmental attitude. He took his ego out of the shot. Swoosh, down the middle and long, at least for Dennis, 225 yards.

GOAL SETTING

We will be looking more at the zone and how to create it later. At the moment, it is more important to get a better understanding of what we have just observed on the 18th tee in the minds of our four golfers. We analyzed Jim's thought process and realized the importance of goal setting. What goals to set and how to set them is not an easy matter. For example, Jim's goal of hitting his "best" shot actually caused of some of his tension. Goals must have two characteristics in order to be helpful: They must be measurable and they must be under the control of the golfer.

In the six-step process, the **GOAL** should include the acronym **AMB**, standing for **AS MEASURED BY**. The goal of shooting to your handicap is measurable enough, but on a rainy, windy day, not something that you can manage to accomplish no matter what you do. It's the same thing as an intermediate tennis player deciding he

59

wants to return serve especially well one day, not recognizing that he will be facing a Boris Becker serve. He would be wiser to set a goal of swinging smoothly, staying alert and not getting hurt. That is more within his control.

Goal setting can do many things if done correctly. If set high, but not impossibly so, goals make us work harder and learn how to cope with adversity. Playing a tough course, for example, can at first be frustrating, yet later this makes it much easier to deal with playing a difficult layout for the first time. Goals can also map progress. Setting and reaching increasingly more difficult goals documents improvement. Rarely is a goal completely missed, for there is always some way of defining something positive or at least doing part of the task well.

One mental goal we all have is to never experience overwhelming anxiety or humiliation, or uncontrolled pain. We can willingly stride into the lion's den of competition, but the mind's powerful ego-defense mechanisms will automatically defend our psychological sense of well-being. No matter what the circumstance, we want to like ourselves and will do whatever it takes to keep our self-esteem intact, often to the point of doing something foolhardy or stupid. Part of Jim's overswing on the tee was to show his partner how hard he was trying to hit the long ball so that Brent would still like him no matter what the result. The benefit of looking like he was trying hard psychologically outweighed the need for a good swing.

DEFENDING THE REAL, IDEAL AND SOCIAL SELVES

Some social psychologists like to talk about three selves: the real self, the ideal self, and the social self. The real self, of course, is the inside-you, the person you know you are. The ideal self is the way you think you ought to be, but are not. That person we want other people to see and admire is our social self. When Jim cried out after his swing, "Oh man! I pulled it. How could I be so stupid?!?" he was actually expressing all three selves. The real self, which just made a stupid error, needed ego protection. This real self, which felt foolish, was expressing that it knew that it was stupid—no one had to tell him. Saying this helps us to save face. For it is far better to call ourselves stupid than to find out later everyone thought we were but we didn't know it.

The ideal self was also expressed in the statement, "How could I be so stupid?!" Jim hoped this exclamation conveyed the idea that "I am really a much better golfer than this." By the same statement, the social self was now defined as one who knows it has made a mistake, is actually a much better golfer and is appropriately aghast at such a surprising and unusual occurrence taking place. By the vehicle of these defenses, the real self is not a bad and stupid golfer, but a knowledgeable victim of temporary insanity or bad karma.

We have many defense mechanisms to use when our self-esteem is under attack, as it so often is in golf. Keep in mind that the ego does not need defense against an outside danger. The fight-or-flight response is what we use for outside threats, real or imagined. Humiliation and psychological pain are what we defend ourselves against. Imagine having just missed a two-foot putt on the 4th green and now you have a similar putt on the 5th. Your pride is at stake. You miss again. You are humiliated in front of your friends. Your ego is bruised. You can:

1. Say, "I didn't really try."

2. Say, "I pulled it."

3. Complain about a spike mark

4. Quickly fantasize about how well you played last week

5. Say, "No big deal."

6. Complain about the noise in the background

7. Call yourself all sorts of bad names

8. Blame bad alignment, etc.

All of these are defenses against hurting the real self. These defenses are certainly necessary, for without them, none of our egos could take the chance of going out on the golf course. But since we do have them and they work well toward our goal of not feeling inadequate or bad or stupid, we need to keep in mind that they also blind us to reality and, worse, set us up to often seek the wrong goal.

61

Excuses do two things: help us to avoid feeling bad when we make a mistake and help us to avoid trying hard when we're not sure we can succeed.

MARK THE GOLFER

Mark is a respected pro, playing on the tour for a dozen years. He has a tendency to hook the ball as well as the full complement of ego defense mechanisms to protect him when he does. So far on his round today, he hasn't hit it off the world but he expects something to show up at any time. On the 9th tee he needs to hit it long and on the short grass. Mark holds his driver gently, hoping that it is still his friend. Out of the twenty-odd goals we could list offhand, Mark has two of importance to us at this particular moment. The current primary golf goal is to make par and shoot a thirty-four.

[**The omnipresent ego goal is to save face.**]

Mark hits, and there it goes, turning hard left as if directed by ground control. He turns around and glares at the gallery. It was obvious that their breathing distracted him. This little mental tactic saves his ego this time but also sets him up with a built-in excuse next time. Whenever you have strong built-in bail-out methods, you will have an increased tendency to use them, even while you swing. This means that the mind is not focused only on the golf goal but also on how it can make sure an excuse is at the ready. No matter what your level of play....

[**The mind is much more interested in saving the ego than in shooting par.**]

CONTROL

We humans are funny creatures when we tee up on number 1. We go looking for trouble like toddlers chasing the cat. If we stayed at home sipping an iced tea and just imagined playing, we could

62

eagle every hole. But we go out to where we have little control, and then try to pretend all sorts of things to protect our egos, which we have placed under constant threat.

Mark's glare at the gallery was a way of protecting his ego after his hook. He knows that it was his fault for hitting it poorly. That doesn't matter very much. Usually we will do almost anything to retain a sense of control and dignity. A quick glare can do a lot to protect the ego and relieve tension and anger. Golf is the kind of game in which achieving mastery is very much up to the internal processes of the player. There is little that can be done to directly defend against the course or the good play of an opponent.

As you know, the mind tries to make sense of things, and that includes golf shots. Bernard Weiner (1972) talked about this issue as one of "locus of control." Where we place the blame for results (like a hook out of bounds) has a lot to do with how we react and how we defend our egos. The diagram below presents the concept. "Internal" are the two factors within our minds and "external" are outside realities and thus not under our direct control.

	INTERNAL	EXTERNAL
STABLE	Level of skill	Difficulty of shot
UNSTABLE	Amount of effort	Luck

Basically, this chart tells us that we have four options for making sense of a good shot or a bad one. Depending on many of the human factors we have discussed, a player can congratulate himself for a good shot by praising his ability or his effort or by deciding that the shot was easy or he was just lucky. Where we place praise or blame makes a lot of difference in feeling good or feeling bad at the result.

If the golfer believes that his effort makes a difference, he will be motivated to practice and seek coaching, whereas an emphasis on natural ability might reduce practice time and analysis of swing mechanics. Nick Faldo is an example of the effort school, Fred Couples of the "leave the ability alone" way of thinking. Many players motivate themselves by defining the task as very difficult, that way arousing their competitive fires to do battle. We certainly have control over effort, some control over our ability and choice of how

63

hard a shot we are willing to try and little but superstitious control over luck (more on luck later).

Look at the chart from your own point of view. Do you think that effort will produce results for you? If so, make sure you don't make the mistake many players do in believing that the harder you work, the better you will get. That was right for Hogan, but it is not the best approach for everyone.

PLACING BLAME

In control of the golf ball or not, we attempt to understand what is happening and are willing to make up reality when needed. We want stability and we want predictability. When we don't have it, we create it. You can hear professionals doing this after hitting into a creek when they could have safely laid up. They rationalize, "I would do it over again; it was the right shot." In this way they are saying that they were under control, things were as they should be, they know the problems and the right solutions. Their locus of control is ability and effort, not that they might have underestimated the difficulty of the task or their readiness to accomplish it. Only later, sometimes years later, will they admit that they made a fundamental mistake and were completely unaware of doing so at the time.

You may see a pro tapping down spike marks after missing a short putt. You have to wonder how much of a problem those particular spike marks were or if he was unconsciously protecting his ego. This is not to say that blaming is bad. Often saving the ego this way allows the player to continue to play his best. It is usually better to blame something outside your control than to blame yourself. Except that the very best are always looking for errors or weaknesses in order to improve. To play your absolute best, you must always be on the lookout for personal faults in both the physical and mental game.

$$\left[\text{The idea is to keep your ego out of errors.}\right]$$

Let's apply this idea to Mark. After his terrible hook, he glared at the gallery. He automatically assumed that his ability and his effort were sufficient. Only the gallery noise distracted him and made the task impossible. Or, he may be sensing that he was a victim

64

of bad luck because the gallery made a noise at the wrong time. In either case, the task was impossible and therefore he is innocent of poor play. If Mark blamed the poor shot on his tendency to hook, his ability would be called into question. Obviously this would cause all sorts of problems in confidence and effort.

How about another situation where the fairway was very narrow but he decided to hit his driver anyway for a chance at an easy birdie? He could place the locus of control over his bad shot in:

EXTERNAL/STABLE (DIFFICULTY OF SHOT)

The fairway was just too narrow to hit no matter what club he may have decided to use off the tee.

EXTERNAL/UNSTABLE (LUCK)

It was just bad luck that his otherwise good shot had to land in a very thick part of the rough just off the fairway.

INTERNAL/STABLE (SKILL)

He was simply not good enough with the driver to attempt a big tee shot to such a narrow landing area.

INTERNAL/UNSTABLE (EFFORT)

He didn't take into account all the factors. The architect fooled him into choosing his normal driver on a long par-4 and he hurried his swing just to get it over with.

There are many ways a player can interpret the events. Keep in mind that how Mark reacts (and how you do) depends on the perception of these things, not necessarily on their reality.

The concept is that you will blame one of these factors for your errors. There is no simple best way to perform a task, but there are ways to mess it up. Blaming your ability too much becomes discouraging. Blaming luck too much, though, means that you are not looking for errors and potential solutions from within yourself. The idea is to define each element as accurately as possible. A good player or teacher is aware of these locus-of-control factors because they have a lot to do with ego defense, goal setting, motivation and coping with frustration.

65

For example, if a 13 handicap expected to play his long irons consistently well, he would be setting himself up for disappointment. Recognizing that his internal/stable ability is only moderate, he could set personal goals that are appropriate and motivating, such as hitting acceptable 3-irons half the time. He would then avoid the need for ego defenses since he would not be attempting things outside his ability to achieve. He would also know how to set goals high enough to continue his improvement. Knowledge of these four elements helps the player to keep his game in perspective.

Here is an example of locus-of-control factors for my usual casual game with friends.

	INTERNAL	EXTERNAL
STABLE	My skill level is good but aging a bit	No shot is too difficult to try
UNSTABLE	Trying hard isn't a lot of fun	Bad luck only adds to the fun of challenge

You might be able to guess from my chart that I usually play for fun with my friends, don't mind losing much to them and would rather have one spectacular shot in a round than to string together five conservative pars. This "locus of control" is for casual golf, to keep the focus on fun. Competitive rounds, however, are a different matter because self-esteem and the outcome of the match are more at risk.

LEARNED HELPLESSNESS

One other concept that I want to touch on here is something called "learned helplessness." In animal studies in which dogs are shocked with small jolts of electricity or rats are placed in water-filled barrels with neither having a chance to escape, researchers found that these animals would soon give up trying to get away and passively accept whatever happened to them. Their attitude seemed to become, "Why fight it if I can't do anything about it?" We golfers tend to get into this frame of mind sometimes when our ability is not

66

up to the task, luck has been against us or we are too tired or otherwise have lost our motivation. This is a normal response to a situation we feel is no longer under our control.

Some people never get to this point. They are always certain that something can be done. These strong-willed individuals seek strength from inside themselves or keep looking for some solution in the situation that has been overlooked. Walter Hagen, Ben Hogan, Gary Player and Raymond Floyd are some names that quickly come to mind. Others throw in the towel at the first hint of trouble, preferring to blame the difficulty of the task or bad luck. These players would rather face a sense of helplessness or doom than risk trying harder and still failing. You probably know people of both types, and you lean one way or the other yourself.

THE BEST PLAYERS

This basic attitude colors how we define problems and our responsibility to resolve them. What situations you attempt, like playing difficult courses, and how hard you try, depends on how much risk you are comfortable taking. We are not talking about risk in the sense of going for a tight pin placement, but in the sense of risking self-esteem. The best golfers enjoy the risk and take on greater and greater tasks. Nick Faldo's completely revamping his swing in mid-career is a good example. These players are able to accept personal responsibility for success or failure. What enables them to do this is their defining the game as competition, against the course, an opponent or themselves. The chance to win any of these competitions whets the appetite.

The best athletes have low degrees of tension, which means that they don't worry too much about the externals, luck and task difficulty, things outside their control. They concentrate on internals, working hard and trying to improve. They are assertive, self-sufficient, strong-minded. The very best are always critically evaluating their performance, looking for flaws that can be fixed. Self-worth is a given, but they make the contest important and give it their all.

> **The best players place total importance on winning and believe that their effort determines the outcome.**

All the best players have one similar mental key: the desire to do to the **EGO** whatever it takes to succeed. Most importantly, that includes risking self-esteem and accepting failure. In a way they are like race-car drivers, knowing that those behind are willing to drive on the edge of control over life and limb and that they must do likewise to their egos. What top-level golfers do that the rest of us don't is define failure as only a temporary event, soon to be overcome by smarter and better play.

They have all of the mental elements that the rest of us have: the assumptions, the thought processes, the anxious reactions and the defense mechanisms. The elite put it together, however, in a way that is productive rather than restrictive. Ability is seen as unlimited and always ready to be improved. There is no task too difficult if the proper preparation is made and such preparation is the responsibility of the player. Effort is always maximum because the only goal that is important during play is success—not feeling good, not having a fun time nor necessarily being a nice guy. All that can come later, after competition. Luck is defined as only another hazard to be overcome.

THE HALF-BAKED MIND

As you now know, the mind can define the situation in many ways depending on what the individual needs to perceive. For some golfers, being perfect is the only acceptable outcome. The player certainly knows that no one can be perfect at golf, but that does not stop his emotions from overreacting to a mishit or a bad bounce. Blame for failure is usually internal and therefore ego deflating. This is a situation that will eventually lead to burnout. The half-baked mind tends to quick judgments. One poor shot early on means the round is ruined. One miss or bit of misfortune can be overcome but only by uncommon good luck, as if the golf gods were finally looking down with a favoring eye or by an unbroken series of excellent shots that clearly prove that the player can overcome absolutely everything.

Similar to the perfectionist is the player who believes that one bad shot means everything will be bad. This is what we call the "all-or-nothing response." This player could try a difficult hook shot to the green, draw the ball well, yet hit it a little too hard and end up throwing the club into the dirt in disgust. This is also termed "one-trial generalization," as if one time means all the time. For example, a player misses the fairway off the first tee and worries from then on about his driver.

Another approach to control is that of the player who takes everything personally. A bad shot means less self-worth. Sometimes this player will assume everything that happens is aimed at him. The wind affects his game more than anyone else's or the course gives his rivals all the advantage. Others actually believe that golf should be fair! Many of us get overinvolved in blaming something—ourselves, the course or the fates. It is as if a bad shot must be attributed to something or it doesn't make sense. An excess of such an attitude focuses the mind more on regaining control than on producing a golf swing.

All these thoughts and attitudes are attempts to minimize any assault to an ego that perceives the game as significant and potentially damaging. If uncontrollable outside agents are at work, if it isn't our day, if we can't be perfect, if the task is too hard, our minds tell us to pack up our emotional marbles and escape. We do this by actually quitting or in more subtle ways by not trying so hard or (more unconsciously) by missing an important shot. Some of the historic gaffs of the world's greatest players during the tension ridden Ryder Cup attest to this problem. Each one of us has a different definition of when and how this ego protection will occur.

WHAT YOU KNOW NOW

There is a lot more to enjoyable and proficient golf than choosing a club and hitting the ball. The mental process of thinking has built-in assets that can easily become liabilities. Our need to preserve dignity and self-worth is so powerful that the strongest of men and women tremble on the first tee of a Major Championship. These players have hit thousands of similar tee shots, yet the mind says, "Go home before something terrible happens." Whenever we define a goal, such as shooting par on a particular hole, we have the unspoken goal of feeling self-worth despite what happens. Our efforts toward that golf par can be strongly interfered with by our simultaneous efforts to protect our egos.

In order to command the mental game, you must take into account how the mind processes information, in what order and toward what goal. This is where the six-step process can be applied with terrific advantage to all playing situations. Since all of our behavior is goal-oriented, you must be aware of what golf goals and what mental goals your mind has established and how they might interfere with one another. You must be able to find blame for results in a productive way. Because of their extraordinarily powerful ways of ruining our swings, the ego's defense mechanisms must also be noted and rectified. Last, methods to cope with our natural fear reactions must be used so that we can confidently stand over a shot, despite the threat of attack from that saber-toothed tiger creeping up behind us.

7

ON THE COURSE

eality, for the mental game, is not the primary hazard as it is for the physical game. As you have learned, the mind will change reality in order to feel safe, secure and happy. This is the mind's mental par, always the goal and always more important than par on the course. When I first played golf, I easily scored in the low eighties. I did this by not counting missed shots I could have made if the grass hadn't been bumpy, if there hadn't been a noise—after all, I made it last time, and so on. I used any one of the many ego defense mechanisms to write down the score my mental game needed to see. We all do this in our club selection, the tees we play from, the clothes we wear, the players we admire and in the definition we have in our heads of our "real" golf game.

Our mental game is made up from our belief system, our mental capacities and the needs of our ego. We are all fully capable of shooting triple bogeys on the real course in order to enjoy a par in our minds. Take, for instance, a tour player who is in contention, playing a par-3 like the 12th at Augusta with water in front of the green. His first ball is wet and he tees up a second. His mind is agonizing over his receding chance of victory. If he hits a good shot now, and birdies in, he has a chance. For some golfers in this situation, one mental par is defined by never giving up. This player will continue to try hard, no matter how discouraged he becomes. This player will change his club to a longer one or aim at the fat of the green, accepting that he has misjudged the shot and given one away.

Many players have a different par, one that is to avoid looking like they have made a mistake. This kind of player might hit another one or two balls into the water before he successfully reaches the green. He continues this seemingly insane behavior because he must hit the club he first chose to prove that it was the correct choice.

A third kind of response would be to unconsciously give up, scoring big numbers on the rest of the holes to prove that "fate was against me," luck being the primary locus of control for this player. Or, in a kind of perverted logic, high scores could be described to fellow competitors in the locker room later almost as a "red badge of courage." Do you see how the reality of the external golf game can be completely controlled by the little one inside our heads?

MENTAL PARS

I did a study once at the Craft-Zavichas Golf School as to why the students played golf. Most of them reported that they played for fun. For the majority of golfers, enjoyment is the "mental par," that is, the ideal accomplishment. Trying hard, concentrating, working at the game are bogeys to them. A second par was companionship. Playing with a friend was more important than defeating an opponent. A competitive attitude seemed to them to feel like a bogey or worse. If an improved game is easy to accomplish, these players will add what is needed, such as using a longer ball, using clubs weighted to help get the ball airborne or taking lessons in a vacation atmosphere. This suggests a third personal par of competence. To be a complete golfer, you need to know how you define your personal mental pars.

I think that there are three mental pars for every golfer, refined by each individual of course, but basic to us all. The first mental par is arousal. That is, a comfortable level of intensity. Created by the individual's definition of the approach-avoidance challenge of the game, this will be higher for some than for others, depending on the person's personality and the situation. The second par is stress level. In order to create the best stress level, appropriate goals are mandatory. Competitors love the stress of being in the hunt over the last nine holes. The last mental par is satisfaction, the enjoyment or fun of playing. This is composed of expectations and a measure of competence. Satisfaction for the high-handicap golfer can be enjoying the companionship or exercise of golf, or the pleasure at the 19th hole of describing a miracle shot in a round of a hundred hacks.

Having an awareness of mental pars will help you meet the combined demands of swinging the club and using your head. Many books on the mental game present the concept that a shot is the same whether for birdie or double bogey. The idea being: the player should recognize that the physical action required to make the shot is identical no matter what the situation. This idea fails to take into account mental par, a far more powerful motivator than making birdie or saving bogey or whatever. Don't make the mistake that pretending something (like you are really confident when you are not) is an adequate tool of the mental game. You cannot pretend that a shot is something different from what it is. Take into account your mental pars and how to achieve them and you will manage the physical game a lot better as a result.

MENTAL HAZARDS*

PART ONE

To achieve mental pars you must overcome mental obstacles. These mental hazards are circumstances, defined by the individual,

---

*Charles W. Moore in 1929 predated my thinking about mental hazards.

that create conflict between internal goals. For example, the drive to succeed can easily come into conflict with the need to avoid embarrassment. The classic "fear of success" syndrome is the problem a person has of fearing that if he wins, he will be expected to win again. Even after he wins once, he fears that if he doesn't manage to win again for a while, there must be something wrong with him or that first win was a fluke and he really isn't that good. Winning for the first time is especially hard because of the mental definition of "belonging" that comes with it. A feeling of belonging is obviously a mental par for tour players. The major hazard is the sense of inadequacy many of them have until they have proven themselves as winners.

Our friend Jim, back on the 18th tee, had an interesting hazard that helped create his bad tee shot. He wanted to win, but was unaware of his mental bunker of also wanting his partner to feel good. Jim's hope that Brent would come through made him a little uncertain, a little hesitant, and as a result, a lot out of bounds.

Many good players don't concentrate enough on easy shots because their mental par of exciting stress is constrained by the mental hazard of too simple a shot. Or the opposite can occur. They play very difficult shots well because the shot difficulty is so high that there is no fear of incompetence and thus no mental hazard. A miss is no big deal—nobody could make the shot—but if he makes it, what a hero!

Probably the deepest, most difficult mental hazard is what is termed the "critical audience." This is the part of the mind that worries about what people will think. Early on it was Dad or Mom, then friends. If you are a tour player, it can be your sponsors, the press, history, or your public image. The critical audience doesn't even have to be there to affect our play. It is the threat of evaluation or criticism that creates anxiety, which in turn makes us question our mental goals and ability to reach them. Unless we have incredible self-confidence, there is always the possibility that someone somewhere can find fault with what we've done. Our personal par of intensity can be abandoned to allow us to tell our critical audience that we really didn't try hard enough but we will next time. It is far better for your ego to fail while under your control than to try your absolute best and be judged by others that your best is still not good enough.

Since there are a thousand and one mental hazards, all personally designed by each of us, I have only introduced the concept

74

here; much more will be discussed later. Your job is to keep in mind that the mental hazards are conflicts blocking you from reaching your various mental goals. One last kind, though, is common enough to us all to make it worth discussing. We talked about it briefly when we looked at areas under our control and the concept of learned helplessness.

How a person defines locus of control is another mental hazard. Players who fall into this trap decide that some situations cannot be controlled and give way to luck, then blame bad luck. An example of this is the good player playing a short par 4 that is reachable with a big tee shot, say, like the 280-yard 10th at the Belfrey in England which is protected by water to the front and left. This golfer hits hard and hopes for the best, falling into the mental hazard of "I'll hit and take my chances." Often this player thinks he was robbed if the result is not good. A smart player avoids this problem by accepting responsibility for all the possible bounces of the ball, makes plans for all likely outcomes and is willing to face whatever trouble he may encounter. The guy who played "hit and hope," now in the water, saves his personal par of competence by blaming the bad bounce of an otherwise fantastic tee shot. This player is in the nonproductive excuse-making mode, while the guy who studied all the possible mental hazards is more apt to be writing down a very satisfying three on the card, making a mental par and a real-life birdie. (For the curious who may have thought about it, I don't think that there are such things as mental birdies. The mental game is complicated enough with just pars and bogeys.)

THE MENTAL CLUBS

Now that you have been briefly introduced to mental pars and hazards, we should take a look at mental clubs, your tools to shoot mental pars and avoid the bogeys. You have four major ones: patience, confidence, concentration and acceptance. Think of them as your mental driver, 1-iron, pitching wedge and putter. Each must be carried at all times and used when appropriate. Just as you don't have to hit perfect shots to make par, you do not have to have infinite patience, super confidence, or unwavering concentration, nor do you need to be complacent in order to play your best. What we are talking about is having skills in your own mental game that complement one another and translate to good golf. Attitude is another mental club, as is persistence. Since these are well discussed elsewhere, we will look at only these four primary mental clubs.

PATIENCE

Do you have any idea who has the most patience in golf today? Trick question. The answer is, and always will be, the golf course. It just sits there, pretty as can be, waiting for you to do your best. It gladly rewards good shots and thoughtful play, and gleefully teases by rebounding errant shots back into the fairway or allowing overly strong chips to crash against the pin and fall into the hole. Punishment is swift and certain, however, for bad shots and inadequate thinking. At least we think that the golf course does this to us. Actually, the course doesn't care. It does sit there, pretty as can be, but that's it. The course is neither for us nor against us. Like the universe, it just is. We, in our minds, create the situation of us-against-the-course. And if we keep this attitude, like playing the slots in Las Vegas, eventually we will lose far more often than we win.

Patience is our club for playing the mental course and coping with bogeys in our minds and on the card. Patience is the oil that smooths the troubled waters. It is the balm for bad hits, the medicine that . . . alright already, so how do I get this doggone patience? First you have to understand what impatience is. We get impatient when we don't yet have what we want. So to have patience, we must already have what we want or know we can get it within an acceptable length of time. Simple, right? Take the golfer who likes to play fast and is now playing behind the slowest group on the course. He will lose his patience because he is not getting what he wants, a quick pace. In order to employ the tool of patience and not be constantly frustrated by the slow group in front, he must somehow create what he wants. He cannot pretend to have it, nor can he play well without it. Yet, the conditions are against him.

For the fast golfer, having patience requires playing quickly. If he doesn't have it in his walk to the ball, he must create the same sensation in other ways. One thing he could do would be to hesitate after a shot, keeping his mind occupied with putting his club away, taking to a fellow player or whatever. He could do all this in order to

76

delay being ready to hit until he was able to go through his preshot routine at his normal speed. On an approach shot for example, he could be twenty yards behind his ball when the green cleared, then comfortably "rush" his shot to both fit his own tempo and keep up the pace of play.

Patience means being in control of your reactions, tempo, goals and expectations. You can achieve having what you want by first making sure that what you want can be done. Good goal-setting is the key to this. If you have a fast tempo and are playing a notoriously slow course, you could be setting up a mental hazard for yourself. If you keep your normal goal of playing quickly, you will fall headlong into a deep trap of your own making while the course just sits there astonished at your lack of good sense. Play a good mental game by assessing your goals so you can plan how to reach them. I know that none of you readers would try to hit a driver over water if you were sure you could never make it. Creating reachable mental goals is the same thing. Patience is created when you do it right.

CONFIDENCE

T he second mental club is confidence. Confidence is the feeling that you can accomplish something. The trick here is to understand what is to be accomplished. *It is not a good golf shot or a good golf score.* This is a book on the mental game and I want you to think mental. What is important in confidence is again how the player interprets the event, not the event itself. Is confidence developed by a tour player hitting 220-yard tee shots? No. But how about if a short hitter started to hit them that far? Confidence is built on the individual's learning to expect a positive outcome to a goal defined by his ego as important.

You cannot pretend to have confidence and you can't get it by reading a book.

[**Confidence has to be experienced in order to exist.**]

You can, however, create experiences that will enhance your confidence. Many players end a putting practice by sinking twenty short putts in a row. Having experienced this success makes them feel positive. Another way of doing this is to measure parts of what you wanted to achieve, not simply whether you experienced success or failure. If you didn't win, did you play better? Are you hitting the ball straighter, learning something, getting more pars or concentrating longer? Make sure you are measuring correctly.

Golf is an exacting game. The club must descend at a hundred miles an hour to a spot under the ball that many of us can't see without our glasses. Our beginning golfer Judi in Chapter Three had no confidence because she didn't know how to measure her accomplishments. In order to carry confidence in your mental bag you must create experiences that enable you to enjoy success and then build increasing challenges that encourage your continued efforts and measure your improvement.

CONCENTRATION

The third mental club, concentration, is best understood as something other than a mental activity. Most people think of concentration as focusing thoughts on something, and they're right. But when a person concentrates by trying to focus attention, it can't be done. Telling yourself to concentrate ends up with you concentrating on thinking, not on the task at hand. Concentration is actually passive, not something you can make happen. Concentration is like happiness. You cannot simply decide to be happy. You do something that ends up making you happy. As with happiness and confidence, you can create a situation that enhances concentration. For our purposes, we may define concentration as the focus on a behavior or feeling.

A number of years ago, when I considered myself a good tennis player, I encountered a fellow with a blinding fast serve. Knowing this before the match, I waited for his first delivery, telling myself to "concentrate, concentrate" in order to be ready. Bam! Ace number one. I moved to the add court. Got ready, "concentrate, concentrate." Bam! Ace number two. Two aces later, while walking to the other court for my own serve, I recalled a coach telling me to focus on seeing the server's toss at the top of the arc. "See the ball being hit while you're on your toes," was his advice. I'm glad to report that the booming server did not ace me again. Instead of trying to concentrate, I focused on seeing the ball and being on my toes.

This enabled my body to react much more quickly than my mind allowed when it was so busy thinking about concentrating.

The sports psychologist Robert Neideffer talks about four kinds of focusing: wide, narrow, external and internal. For example, in football, the quarterback needs a wide external focus of attention to know where all his receivers are. Chess players would do well with wide internal attention. A narrow external focus is helpful for surgeons, while a narrow internal attention is best for something like hypnosis. We need all four for good golf. Below is an example of how the four kinds of attending (focusing) can be employed in golf. Some people can naturally focus in one way better than another. This must be taken into account when you are playing in the same way that you might compensate for a weak long-iron game with additional fairway woods.

	EXTERNAL	INTERNAL
WIDE	Know where you stand in the tournament	Sense all the areas of physical tension
NARROW	Focus on alignment	Key on feeling the finish of the backswing

For example, some players with stronger wide external view would be smart not to look at a leader board until late in the round. These players may have difficulty refocusing on narrower areas like stroking a putt.

Concentration is not just one thing. There are different kinds of focusing, there are individual differences and our ability varies from time to time and situation to situation. To concentrate, you simply pay attention to the task you want to complete. Using my experience again as an example, I had the pleasure one year of playing in the Tournament of Champions Pro Am at La Costa. Talk about a new experience being overwhelming! I was so nervous that my friends had to drag me out of the portable toilet to make our starting time. Although our Pro, Wayne Grady, was as gracious as could be, I was trembling to the degree that it took two hands and three tries while on my knees to balance my ball on the tee. In my mental bag, however, I had polished up my mental clubs.

My patience was defined by my decision to give myself the

79

entire front nine to get relaxed. Our back nine was on the tournament course, so I could more easily forgive myself for misses early on. I wanted to play well on the course I would later see on TV. Hacks, nerves, yips, I would endure them all on the front nine. My primary mental goal was to enjoy the experience. (Golf goals were to hit a good shot off the first tee, make one birdie and outdrive the professional one time.) My confidence was high, too, based on some practicing I had done earlier. I knew I couldn't become a scratch player in the weeks before the tournament. Since it was a best-ball format, I would rarely, if ever, need recovery shots. So I practiced approach shots. Over and over I hit 7-, 8- and 9-irons. I was as good with those as I had ever been. I was ready with at least part of my game. I knew what would be good and could lower my expectations for the rest of my game if I needed to.

I achieved concentration in the same way I established a sense of confidence. I wanted to feel each swing the same as I did when I hit my 7-iron. I had that 7-iron feel firmly entrenched in my mind. So all I did to concentrate was focus on feeling that 7-iron swing. Once I managed to get the ball teed on that first hole, I went through a preshot routine, exhaled and swung my 3-wood like a 7-iron, and hit a wonderful shot down the right center.

ACCEPTANCE

Some of you negative thinkers out there might be wondering how I would have handled a topped shot that was short of the Ladies' tee. So let's talk about acceptance, the fourth mental club. Acceptance is like patience—only it requires a shorter length of time and relates to a specific event. And, as always, the event is a mental one, rather than an external event as you might think. Acceptance refers to one's own failings and limitations, not to coping with a bad shot or losing a match. Few people would mind losing if they had played their best ever, so it isn't losing that is the issue; it is the blow to self-esteem in losing to someone we think we should beat that requires acceptance.

It is interesting to me, as we have discussed, why we play golf when we know that so often the results are destructive to our pride and dignity. Many pros talk about feeling they finally belong on the tour only after their first win, a very difficult feat indeed. We amateurs often measure our worth in increments of breaking a hundred, then ninety and so on. Failing to win or never making a par seems to suggest a weakness or a flaw in character. Rage is often the response when the ball is left in the bunker or the putt comes up just short. Otherwise compassionate individuals become self-destructive monsters after a three-putt, calling themselves unprintable names, as if they had just committed the unpardonable sin.

To add acceptance to your mental bag, you must first find out how your self-esteem is involved in golf. For the most part, the measurement of ego golf is your own particular definition of mental par. Then you must figure out the mental hazards that you create that get in your way. Once you do this, you will have a fair idea of what will drive you crazy on the golf course and can plan to avoid it.

The experience Robert Gamez had on the first tee of the 1990 British Open is a terrific example of acceptance. Picture this young player over for the Open: foreign country, strange food, Major tournament, knowlegeable gallery, the first tee of the Old Course, the Royal and Ancient Clubhouse behind him. His name is called. He goes through his preshot routine. He sets up to the ball and swings, and "clunk," dead-tops it a hundred yards.

Of all the things his mind wanted him to do, including escaping back into the clubhouse, what he did was smile (a rueful smile), walk to his ball, and put such a sweet swing on a long iron that he gave himself a makable birdie putt. He accepted the responsibility of his tee shot, then did what he had to do to hit a good approach.

The idea is to know what you are responsible for, do what you can do, then you can take what you get. This is a version of the formula F=E-R, where you can accept the Results by defining your area of responsibility beforehand.

So what would I have done if my tee shot at the Tournament of Champions was topped short of the Ladies' tee? My plan was to first remind myself that the tension and agony of tournament play was what I was after. Then, in order to protect my real self and social self I was going to say out loud, "I was afraid of that." Then I was going to pick up my ball and cheer my teammates as they went on to finish the hole. Don't ask me what I would have done if I had messed up on the next tee shot. The mental game can't make a good game out of thin air.

EXAMINATION

I want to see how much of the mental game you have been absorbing. So, I have devised this one question test to find out. Here's a hint so you will do well. If you have heard anything about Zen philosophy, you probably have come across the question, "What is the sound of one hand clapping?" According to the Zen approach, you should look at this question directly, not analyzing what it means, but respond to the question by noting your immediate experience. I would like you to approach this golf question the same way. Ready? Here we go:

How long is a three-foot putt?

What did you answer? Since I can't hear you, I will assume you said either "I don't understand the question," "Three feet," or "It depends."

"A's" for all of you who answered "It depends." If you are facing a three-foot putt, one of your minibrains notes its length. Other minibrains may be aware of how scary it is, how important it is, or how tired you are. Shouldn't these factors also be taken into account when you measure a putt? I think so. That's why the correct answer is "It depends."

Although this may be oversimplified, I think the best measure of a golf shot may be in two parts: the physical elements, like distance and direction, and the mental portions, let's call them "psyche" units. For example, a physical three-foot straight-uphill putt for fifty cents might have two "psyche" units, while the same putt for the club championship could be fifty "psyche" units long. The very same putt for the Open Championship might very well have a thousand "psyche" units, especially if the player had never won anything close to that before. If you accept this extra measure, you will not have to pretend anything, just take the extra "psyche" length into account and employ the necessary parts of your mental game. For a golf shot ten yards farther you take one club more. For a shot of more "psyche" units, you use more clubs from your mental bag. Speaking of that, let's venture more into your personal mental game.

8

'OUR MENTAL BAGGAGE

ne of the reasons for the existence of this book is to make sure golfers who want to achieve the most they can from the game have a way of doing so. My point of view is that all of us have certain things we want to gain from our play, from enjoyment of a quick late-afternoon nine holes to winning a major championship. No matter why you play this remarkable game, if you can define your goals, create methods to reach them and know that you are doing so in the most effective way possible, you will be doing all you can to fulfill your expectations. To have this happen, you must be able to evaluate your needs accurately, making sure you are defining a problem that really exists. Second, you must put this problem into perspective. Lamenting that you need more distance does not suggest that the goal should be interpreted as hitting 300-yard tee shots. Last, after the problem and goals are defined, you must construct a framework that allows you to identify the most likely solution strategies. Obviously, the six-step process we have already discussed does this well. Let's use it to identify your personal problem areas.

No book is going to give you all the answers or even ask all the right questions. If what I say or how I say it doesn't make sense to you, it may be that I'm wrong in some of my assumptions about your game and needs. What I know isn't important. What we are after is for you to learn how to use your mind to help you play your best golf. We are after wisdom, not just improved technique. If you don't agree with some of what I say, know why, and what to do for yourself. I want you to know the mental fundamentals as I understand them, but I also want you to be able to take your mental game way beyond the fundamentals. But first . . .

Another Test

	TRUE	FALSE
1. Your conscious and unconscious minds can have different goals.	————	————
2. Saving bogey is a conscious goal.	————	————
3. Saving face can be an unconscious goal.	————	————
4. Stress on Tuesday can affect your play on Saturday.	————	————
5. Your play is affected by other peoples' expectations.	————	————
6. Your unconscious mind is more powerful than your conscious mind.	————	————
7. Stress is a motivator.	————	————
8. Having fun can improve your play.	————	————
9. Having fun can cause you to play worse.	————	————
10. Tension is not caused by outside distractions.	————	————
11. Reaching a goal is the only way to feel satisfied.	————	————
12. A hole is difficult only because of our expectations.	————	————
13. Self-esteem is a mental par.	————	————
14. Liking a hole helps you play it better.	————	————
15. Patience and enjoyment are almost the same.	————	————
16. Your interpretation of what happened is more important than what really happened.	————	————

84

	TRUE	FALSE
17. *The mind thinks that the feeling of anxiety is the signal to do something and quick.*	————	————
18. *Trying too hard is counterproductive.*	————	————
19. *Once you get frustrated, you are more likely to get more frustrated than less frustrated.*	————	————
20. *To play your best, knowing your mind is more important than knowing your swing.*	————	————

All the statements are true. How did you do?

When I give this test to my students, certain questions seem to cause small riots of disagreement, eleven and twelve especially. Number five about playing to others' expectations has to do with the "critical audience" concept. We all have such an audience in our heads, and to the degree we worry about their response, we are not thinking about our golf game.

The questions about stress being a motivator and fun, both helping and hindering our play (questions 7–9), point out how the difficulty and the enjoyment of the task have a great deal to do with how hard we try. Too easy or too much fun and we lose focus, too hard or not fun and we tend to get distracted by our emotional reactions.

Ten, eleven and twelve get me into real hot water. Ten says that our response to distractions is the culprit, not the distraction itself. If a noise distracts you and you tighten up, but you are able to regroup and hit the shot, that is no different mentally than looking at the line of a putt, getting set, then looking at the line again because you are not sure yet of how the ball will break. If, however, you get mad over a distraction, it is your own response that will disrupt your concentration. You, in effect, are distracting yourself.

The pot ready to cook me alive begins to boil with number eleven. Many students say something like, "I can want to get par on a hole, but if I play well and only bad luck or something like that causes me to bogey, I can still feel satisfied that I played the hole as well as I could." Agreed. What these students forget is the difference between a golf par and a mental par. Both a golf par and a mental par are goals. Reaching either goal, or par, will result in the player's feeling satisfied. In the students' example, golf par wasn't reached and the mental par was. But be sure to remember that mental pars are far more important to you than a mere golf par.

85

The twelfth question is the one that has the students ready to hurl me into the pot of boiling water. As they storm toward me, fists upraised, they cry, how can you say "A hole is difficult only because of our expectations?" Now encircling me, one says, "What about a 900-mile par-5, isn't that difficult?" Another shouts, "You can't say the weather doesn't make things harder!" To these outraged, homicidal golfers, I reply from behind and below my desk, that if one attempted to play a 900-mile par-5 in par, then one's expectations clearly are misguided. Just as par is a relative number depending on conditions, so should our expectations reflect the reality of our ability and the demands of the hole. Expecting par on such a hole is ludicrous and proof of my point.

This comment usually brings the mob up short. However, often there are ringleaders still after my hide. It isn't the "only thing" they say. "It may be a significant factor, but it isn't the 'only' cause of difficulty." I almost agree with this, but then I go to the question about our interpretation of reality being more important than reality. You agreed with that, didn't you? Well, some of my students didn't. But remember that, in our minds, we do interpret what we see. An easy hole for you might be a hard one for me. Hard for me because I haven't played it well, or because it requires shots that I don't have. Same hole, different interpretation. If I expect to play it the same as you do, I'm increasing the chances of being disappointed and defining the hole as hard. It would not be a hard hole for me if I defined it as a bogey hole for me and approached it with that mental attitude. Much of your mental game is how you define you and the game you play.

This chapter will help you define your mental golf game so you will know what areas need improvement. Since we now know how the mind works, let's use this knowledge to approach how we define our individual mental games. Because we will again follow the "six-step process to solve every problem," we first need to define the issues. By filling out the following questionnaires you will construct a profile of your personal mental game from which you will then define specific goals. As I mentioned earlier, I cannot uncover or define the subtleties of your mental game, but we can get a fairly good look at some of the important elements. This is a fundamentals book designed only to give you a good start. Keep in mind that there are good professionals out there if you want to follow up on what we begin.

86

There are a number of tests, some specific to golf and others concerning sports in general, that are used to identify individual issues. The Competitive Golf Stress Inventory (CGSI) is a method to measure anxiety during golf competition, for example. For general sports, the Sport Motivation Scales are used in many activities to identify personality factors such as competence and aggression. Many of these tests are well researched and are valid and reliable, especially when administered by a sports psychologist or coach. If you desire detailed and specific analysis of your mental issues, you can consult these experts to good advantage. The book by Andrew Ostrow in the Bibliography describes many of these tests.

The questionnaires included in this section are not so scientific, but were designed to initiate the process of identifying personal issues. Answer the questions as honestly as you can, and review them periodically so you can update them as needed. Each issue you identify can be put into the problem-solving process in the same way I approached the example you will see a little later.

Reason to Play Questionnaire

Number in order of preference the top five reasons you play golf.

Competition _____
Enjoyment _____
Companionship _____
Exercise _____
Learn skill _____
Challenge _____
Relaxation _____
Income _____
Winning _____
Other

_____ _____
_____ _____

List the top two here:

_____
_____

If you feel your golf meets these general standards, go on to the next questionnaire. If not, what do you think is the problem?

_____

_____

_____

_____

Keep this statement in mind when you think about issues and goals.

Golf Anxiety Questionnaire

	TRUE	FALSE
1. *I worry about my first tee shot of the day.*	_____	_____
2. *People watching makes me anxious.*	_____	_____
3. *I lose my feel at the worst times.*	_____	_____
4. *I try to avoid using some of my clubs.*	_____	_____
5. *I have a lot of negative thoughts.*	_____	_____
6. *I think about missing too much.*	_____	_____
7. *Sometimes I "blank out" on a shot.*	_____	_____
8. *I am too hard on myself.*	_____	_____
9. *I tend to overreact sometimes.*	_____	_____
10. *I "rush" my shot too often.*	_____	_____

Obviously the more "Trues" you have, the more anxiety and tension affect your game. If you list more than five answers as "True," anxiety is an large problem for you. Anxiety is a factor for most of us at one time or another, no matter what your score on this test; if you believe it is a negative factor in your play, it probably is. Similar to anxiety is another form of tension caused by expectations and needs not being met.

88

Golf Tension Questionnaire

	TRUE	FALSE
1. *I hate disorganization or incompetence.*	_____	_____
2. *I don't like to be the worst player in my group.*	_____	_____
3. *I try to hurry if my group is slow.*	_____	_____
4. *Others' not knowing golf etiquette bothers me.*	_____	_____
5. *I'd much rather play with friends than with people I don't know.*	_____	_____
6. *I'm unsure of what to do when I play at a new club or a new course.*	_____	_____
7. *Slow play drives me crazy.*	_____	_____
8. *I usually handle the flagstick more than my fellow players.*	_____	_____
9. *I tend to "get out of the way" if I'm playing poorly and my companions are playing well.*	_____	_____
10. *Sometimes a round simply isn't fun.*	_____	_____

A score of five or more "Trues" again means there may be a problem. For those of us who are "course monitors," the behavior of others or our own sense of inadequacy can often cause the tension that makes things worse. If your score or your own sense defines you as a golf course or critical self-monitor, list this as one of your issues.

There is another type of problem, a physical response to anxiety or tension, that creates difficulties for the golfer. When we try too hard, are distracted or worried, are angry, frustrated, unlucky or have simply swung too many times, our bodies get tense and tired.

When you play, or before a tournament do you:

get sore muscles, especially in
your neck or shoulders

have difficulty getting relaxed

suffer headaches

get an upset stomach

feel speeded up

feel tense

drink or smoke to relax

89

have problems getting to sleep or

staying asleep before a big match?

If any of these describe you, your body may be too tense to play good golf. Some degree of tension is necessary, of course, to hit the ball well. The problem lies in having too much tension in the working (agonistic) muscles, or having tension in the antagonist muscles, which are supposed to be relaxed. A good friend of mine is normally a wired kind of guy who becomes more so on the first tee. He stands at address so long that veins begin to bulge in his forearms. When his muscle tension begins to get high enough to power half of Cincinnati, he swings. But by then his arms are going into spasm, which causes him to shorten his backswing to barely waist height. With maximum effort he lurches his body back to the ball in an attempt to finish his swing. Push slices or topped pull shots are his norm. When he relaxes before his swing or shortens his time at address, his swing, his attitude and his game are beautiful to watch.

If muscle tension may be a factor in your play, list it here and describe where in your body you feel it.

_____

_____

OTHER ISSUES

Other mental areas that may be issues in your play need to be identified. Below are characteristics that apply to all of us to some degree. If you feel that any apply to you and your golf game, mark an "x" next to the characteristic and add it to your problem list.

1. *I tend to give up too soon.*   _____
2. *I don't like competition.*   _____
3. *Practice isn't enjoyable for me.*   _____
4. *I don't like to admit being wrong.*   _____
5. *I get distracted too easily.*   _____
6. *Bad luck really disturbs me.*   _____
7. *I have a negative attitude.*   _____
8. *I don't think about course management.*   _____

90

9. *I try too many miracle shots.* _____
10. *I don't work hard at improving my game.* _____
11. *I am not very mentally "tough."* _____
12. *I'd rather enjoy myself than win.* _____
13. *I always seem to have an excuse.* _____
14. *After a miss, I have to blame something.* _____
15. *I'm afraid of losing so I don't play in some events.* _____
16. *I don't have enough confidence in myself.* _____
17. *I choke too easily.* _____
18. *I criticize myself after a bad shot.* _____
19. *One mistake tends to lead to others.* _____
20. *I get jealous of better players.* _____

Other problem areas that apply to you:

1. _____

2. _____

3. _____

Now that we have listed some or all of your current mental game issues, we must define the goal that is most appropriate for each one. Since these are personal, I can't list here those you should have for yourself. The best I can do is give you an example, so you can figure the right ones for you.

Below I have summarized a typical problem for the touring professional and have defined an appropriate goal. I have also listed the third element in how to solve problems, the obstacles.

A Tour Professional's Dilemma

Why I play golf: *Make a living*
Competition

Identified issue: *I don't concentrate well if I know I'm out of contention or will not make the cut.*

Goal: *To play to my best ability all the time as measured by feeling fully focused before every shot.*

91

Obstacles:	*I am not highly motivated to do this.*
	Not being in contention reduces
	my desire to try hard.
	Concentrating is very difficult if
	there is no reward.
	I feel like I'm wasting my time.
	Etc.

Got the idea? For each of your issues, you will need to define a measurable goal and list all those things you can think of that might stop you from reaching it. Later we will apply the same techniques to course management and shot selection, as well as make sure you can apply it to your mental game as a whole.

When you do this exercise for yourself, make sure you are not saying *how* anything should be done. Do not define a problem or goal and sneak in a solution instead. Just define what the problem is and your definition of the goal. We are not looking for solutions at this stage. We are defining the problems and goals in logical, concrete ways so as to make them as manageable as a grip change.

So far, we have focused on the issues of the mental game in general and identified some of the problem areas.

The next section of the book will describe many of the problem-solving methods that are currently used by athletes in many sports and, of course, by successful golfers. These can be the beginning of your solution list for each of your mental game issues.

9

APPLYING THE BASICS

ow that you know a considerable amount of the theories of golf psychology, I think it's fair to ask you another question: What is the main **issue** of the mental game? Concentration? Relaxation? Positive attitude? Nope. The answer is simply: how to apply the mental game to maximum advantage. How you define maximum advantage will include a number of different things depending on how you define your goals.

Want to try another question? How about: What is the main **goal** of the mental game of golf?

If you answered, "To hit a good golf shot," you're not emphasizing the mental part of the game. It's important to think in mental terms and not in terms of scoring to fully comprehend the psychology of golf. The main goal of the mental game is:

"To be fully prepared to hit the ball." That's all. The mental game is mostly the preparation to hit the ball and a little bit of coping with the results.

Using what you have learned so far, let's take a look at how Terri, a third-year player on the LPGA tour, applies the concept of issues and goals to her specific situation. She's languishing in the second twenty-five on the money list, making a good living but anxious to break into the top ten. She has a good swing, one that stands up to pressure, and is fairly sure that her attitude or some other part of the mental game is holding her back. So Terri decides:

ISSUE: *To apply the mental game to maximum advantage to my career on the tour.*

GOAL: *To be fully prepared for:*
      a. Each tournament
      b. Each shot
      c. Every eventuality
  As measured by:
      Having the feeling of being fully prepared and when I make a mistake, having the self-esteem to accept it and the knowledge that I can figure out how to fix it.

This is a great start in constructing a functional mental game. Naturally, her goal of being fully prepared will require some refinement, which will in turn enable her to measure her success or lack of success more easily and accurately.

Watch Out For Mistakes!

Terri could refine her original issue by defining a second-level problem such as "coping with a bad attitude." Doing so, however, would be a mistake. This is where you have to be very careful because what may seem like a problem may not be. If Terri analyzed her bad attitude, she would soon realize that her attitude is a result of expectations set too high to meet. Her bad attitude is not a secondary issue or problem to be solved but a consequence of poor goal-setting. Failure to meet the goals she set each January has become frustrating and thus, over time, the cause of her bad attitude. Learning to set appropriate goals would be a more accurate and constructive issue for her to have identified. Defining the issue accurately is critically important and one of the major difficulties in

94

constructing a good mental game. Often, it is helpful to discuss the issues with someone who knows you and your game to get an outside opinion of your (as you have learned) fallible perceptions.

Almost all primary issues have second-level, third-level, and sometimes many more subdivisions. Each issue must be defined in relationship to other issues, so that each one is independent and yet a part of a systemized plan. The value of separating issues and goals is to identify problems and goals accurately so that you are not trying to solve a problem that doesn't exist or trying to solve the wrong problem. The best way of making sure this doesn't happen to you is to understand the four elements of smart golf.

THE BIG PICTURE

For the mental game of golf, smart golf is seamless. The theoretical goal is to have the brain and mind in such harmony prior to the swing that the mind/body split is nonexistent and the swing takes place almost without effort or thought. In his wide-ranging and personalized book, *Links*, Lorne Rubenstein explains that the mental complexity of golf stems from its not being a reaction game. In most sports, he says, the game comes to us and we must react, almost without any time to think. This makes us less likely to mess things up by thinking too much. But with golf, the ball sits patiently waiting for us to do something. And while it waits, we think.

Because of this extra time that is available for planning out our strategy and deciding how we are going to hit the ball, all the possible outcomes, from "nailing it on the screws" to "laying carpet over the ball," enter our various minibrains. In addition, since the ball is just sitting there waiting for our best effort, it can be no one's fault but our own if the ball is not hit perfectly. When the shot fails to come off as we expected, we have no one to blame but ourselves.

How many times have you berated yourself after a bad shot? You do that because you don't know better. You think that you screwed up, made a mistake, did something dumb. The shot didn't work, you were at fault, sometimes without your even knowing what went wrong. You wouldn't be so hard on yourself after a mistake if you knew that you were fully prepared and did your absolute best. But, you don't know how to measure that. Now you will.

95

Use the following criteria to measure if you're playing smart golf:

1. CONFIDENCE   You have a positive attitude about your goal, your choice of club, your shot selection and your ability to make the shot.

2. RELAXED INTENSITY   You are feeling balance between your desire (intensity) to make the shot and acceptance of the result.

3. NONJUDGMENTAL ATTITUDE   Your ego and sense of worth are not involved in the shot in spite of your desire to do well.

4. HERE AND NOW   Your attention is focused on the present.

Although these criteria look logical and very much self-evident, they are not so simple to achieve. Even when things are going well, the mind can make reaching these criteria difficult. In 1991, Ian Baker-Finch had been playing well for months prior to the British Open. His good play lasted well into the Championship. During the last round he opened up a massive five-stroke lead. Let's look how each of the mental criteria we've identified can be involved in such a situation.

CONFIDENCE

Confidence, in setting his goals, in making decisions and in his ability was not as simple for Baker-Finch as it might appear. With a large lead, does he play to keep it or to extend it? Does he work to prove to his critical audience that he will not lose a lead again as he had before or focus on his own game and let the field do what it will? Does he hit driver because he has been hitting it well or take a safer 1-iron so as not to be second-guessed after a bad shot? Does he change his goal on some holes to bogey in order to take double bogey out of the picture or keep the same assertive attitude that got him the lead in the first place?

96

RELAXED INTENSITY

Should a player feel the same high intensity with a large lead or allow himself to relax? Television commentator Dave Marr mentioned that Baker-Finch might be better off if someone made a run at him, so he would be inspired to keep up his intensity. What happens is that many players have a competitive comfort zone that stimulates them to play their best. Too far behind or too far in front is like a goal too difficult or too easy—motivation and intensity go down or are focused more on thought than on the game. Although a player like Baker-Finch would probably not lose his intensity in a major tournament, any occurrence that pushes the player outside his competitive comfort zone must be addressed.

NONJUDGMENTAL ATTITUDE

To keep a nonjudgmental attitude with a big lead is also sometimes harder than you might think. What can happen in this situation is that the player's expectations become more critical. For example, with a five-stroke lead, Baker-Finch may have thought that he was doing great as long as the lead didn't dwindle down to two. Losing three strokes of his lead might create significant negative thinking.

Compare this negative definition of a two-stroke lead (down from five strokes) to someone who has been behind all day and suddenly has a chance to tie with a birdie on the 18th. Many players feel it is harder to play not to lose than it is to come from behind. If you are two ahead and losing the lead, the situation feels perilous. If you are two behind and gaining on the lead, it is fantastic. It all has to do with judgmental perspective. Trying and not succeeding is a lot easier on the ego than having the game in your pocket, then losing. Sometimes critical thinking can occur when just a small mistake is made. A bogey after missing the green could be interpreted that the wheels may be about to fall off, especially if the player is way outside his normal scoring comfort zone.

HERE AND NOW

Ian Baker-Finch may have been thinking about his prior collapses during his final eighteen. Or, with a few holes to go, how ecstatic he will be when he wins. He could have been thinking about financial bonuses, his wife's delight or his place in history. Any kind of thinking out of the "here and now" would place his game in jeopardy.

Anything that happens in golf, whether it is wonderful, like having a large lead in the British Open, or terrible, like discovering that you left your putter at home, stimulates your mind and thus inhibits your golf swing. Assume that any change in the situation will affect your mental game. In addition, any difference between what you expect to happen and what actually happens will also influence the pressure you feel and how you think.

Some players are unaware of many changes occurring in the situation and therefore are not as bothered as those who do notice such things. These players can "play their own game" and disregard what others are doing. They feel little need for learning and practicing the mental game because they are not focusing on gathering excess information and thus having to do something with it. These players have few mental hazards that require identification and resolution. For the rest of us, a few more introductory comments on mental hazards is in order.

MENTAL HAZARDS

PART TWO

For the purposes of easy application to the mental game, I have divided the mental hazards into four groups, one of which really doesn't exist. In Chapter Seven, I introduced concepts concerning mental hazards, like the critical audience, for example. Now I would like you to become comfortable with the idea that every change—in the situation, in your body, in your emotions or in your thinking pattern—is a mental hazard. Below are the mental hazards to your game.

The major hazards

    a. Environmental

    b. Physical

    c. Emotional

    d. Cognitive (Thinking)

The one that doesn't exist is the environmental hazard, but I listed it because it needs to be discussed before we eliminate it from consideration. The first two appear to be outside the brain and not part of the mental game. As you may remember and as you will see, it is not what goes on outside your mind that's important, but how your mind interprets the situation and how it reacts to it.

ENVIRONMENTAL HAZARDS

No matter what change occurs, from the weather turning cold, with snowdrifts covering the greens, to your opponent shooting a fifty-eight, the only thing that is important is your unique perception of the event and how you put the event into perspective. The event itself is not important, only your reaction to it. That is why some players have no need to work on the mental game, while others do. The lucky ones have a "Who cares?" attitude that enables them to cope with practically everything. However, some of us notice things and react in ways that are not to our best advantage. These outside events then become stimulants to our other mental hazards.

PHYSICAL HAZARDS

The physical hazards are simple and easy to define. Again, they are any event to which you have to adjust or which is different from what you expected. In this case, anything in your body that requires an adjustment is a physical hazard. Fatigue is the most common example. When I am tired, I tend to hit more quickly and also tend to keep my weight on the right side. It seems like I muscle the ball too, probably because I think I have to. Another common physical hazard is tension.

99

EMOTIONAL HAZARDS

The most common emotional hazard is frustration, with anxiety following close behind. When changes occur, or if the situation is not going as we expected it to, we fall into the multiple bunkers of tension, frustration, anger, anxiety etc.

These are summarized by:

F = E - R (If you've forgotten: Frustration is equal to the difference between expectations and results.)

Our emotional hazards are made up of the powerful drives we have inherited, our expectations and how much we have involved our self-esteem in the outcome. For many players, the emotional hazards are the deepest and most destructive.

COGNITIVE HAZARDS

These are caused by inappropriate information collecting and poor mental processing. A negative mind-set is a cognitive hazard. In fact, a mind-set can be both a mental hazard and a mental club. Confidence is a mind-set. So is thinking that you're a lousy putter.

Before we venture into the details of mental hazards in the next chapter, I'd like you to list some of your own. Often it is helpful to define what you think you know so that you can better measure what you have learned. For many players, their mental hazards are so ingrained that they do not identify them as hazards but rather as a natural occurrence of play.

One pro I know missed more than his share of five-foot putts. He defined the problem as a poor stroke. In fact, he was a good putter. He knew he was a good putter and thus had high expectations on shorter putts. These overly high expectations put more pressure on the makable ones. As he stood over a putt he knew he should make, a far corner of his mind reminded him that these putts can be missed. You know by now that if the mind thinks it, it must be true. Most of his mind was confident, yet that small voice of doubt was

100

also heard. His mind could not feel comfortable with two messages and began the search for a solution. Not finding one, because both minds were correct, he became anxious, and he began to worry about his stroke. His "bad" stroke was caused by a combination of a cognitive and an emotional hazard. With more pressure, he did worse. He thought his way into a problem that really didn't exist.

Let's take a closer look at the real hazards of the mental game of golf.

MENTAL HAZARDS

ow that you know that all hazards—on the course and in our minds—can lead to the same thing, a mental problem, you need to understand how your mind defines them. This chapter will look at many of the hazards of golf in detail. Make sure that you know how you currently approach all of them, and what goals and solutions you have tried in the past. Decide now to change any that need it.

ENVIRONMENTAL

I want to start off by talking again about the mental hazard that doesn't really exist, the environmental hazard. Assume that an environmental hazard is anything outside your body that stops you from playing your best golf, or at least seems in the way of your best golf. Recall Weiner's idea of locus of control? He talked about internal/external and stable/unstable elements, with luck being external and unstable. Something external/unstable is what I mean by an environmental hazard. I want to talk about four of them: luck, distractions, weather and slumps.

For all of them, the key concept to keep in mind is attitude, one of your mental clubs. No matter what the environmental hazard, it exists only because of your reaction to it. For those we will discuss, my goal is for you to be able to identify and then cope with the hazard. Naturally, you will get better and better with practice.

LUCK

Noneofus would care about luck if it were always good luck and always for us. Or would we? Years ago there was a *Twilight Zone* episode on television where a bad guy died and found himself in a place where his luck was always good. He played pool and on the break all the balls went in. Every time, they always went in. In fact, with everything he did, his luck was perfect. He was in heaven. But soon, *all* good luck began to drive him crazy until he realized that he wasn't where he thought he was.

What makes "luck" interesting is that it always has a value to it. Luck is always good or bad, depending on whether the outcome was good for you or bad for you. Luck is never neutral, but it does seem that we expect it to be. In the long run does luck even out? I don't know, but it doesn't matter. Luck doesn't exist until you decide it does. Whenever you create luck, it will soon turn against you.

Bad luck means that just by chance you didn't get what you wanted. So you have two adjustments to make, one to not getting something and the other to the evil randomness of the event. You are frustrated and angry that the luck that could have gone either way went against you. Luck, however, is neither for nor against you. Just like the golf course and the universe, it just is. Luck is important only because we, and our circumstances, put value on it. Since we put value on it, we can just as well take the value out.

If you are a handicap player, you recognize (I hope) that you will hit a fair number of mediocre shots each round. As long as you

103

don't hit too many and have a few good ones, you'll be pretty happy. Even at the professional level, a few misses in a round are fully acceptable. We tend to define luck the same way. A little bad luck here and there tempered with a little good luck is part of the game. But let us suffer "too much" and we feel unfairly victimized. (Too much good luck also seems to raise our suspicions of wondering when the bad luck is going to take over.)

None of us will ever have too much good luck. If we are enjoying a long string of birdies, so be it. Putts will begin to stop short soon enough. Our job with good luck is to avoid second-guessing it. Just go with the flow. With bad luck, the same is true. Don't try to second-guess it. And don't misdefine it, either. Bad luck is not a ball pulled down the tree line, hitting one and bouncing out of bounds. That was a bad shot. Nor is bad luck scorching the hole all day with none of the putts dropping. That was "close but no cigar" putting, not bad luck. In fact, I'm not sure what bad luck is. Maybe bad luck is hitting the "perfect" tee shot and ending up in a deep divot. But that seems more to be part of the unfairness of golf, and we've already agreed that golf is not fair. Maybe bad luck is if someone else enjoys good luck and you don't. See what I mean? Luck is an attitude, something we decide, not something that happens to us.

$$\left[\textbf{Luck is always under your control.} \right]$$

Bad luck is a bad attitude toward a random event like a "bad" bounce. I like the idea of good luck as something we can enjoy every once in a while if we don't worry about it's going away, and bad luck as something we can overcome with a realistic and positive attitude.

WEATHER

Rain, cold, heat, wind, fog and whatever else that can be experienced on the course certainly qualifies as an environmental hazard. Some players love bad weather. They know that bad conditions discourage a large percentage of the field and thus improve the winning chances of those that can adapt. I like marginal weather myself

104

because the course is less likely to be crowded, I have more of a challenge from an easy course and I have a built-in excuse for a bad score. (An added and often accidental benefit can arise when you take a loved one on the course. It rains and gets cold. You cuddle together to stay warm and soon decide to forget golf and return indoors for a romantic dinner and a fire.)

Weather creates a lot of change. Wind throws the ball about, rain causes flyers and skippers, while heat can cause the player to wilt like a dried prune and feel a thousand years old. If you get discouraged when you see that the weather is going to make things difficult, you must keep in mind that your reaction to the conditions is a mental hazard. The weather doesn't care. The weather is neither good nor bad. Like luck, the universe and the golf course, it just is. The weather says, "I'm here, figure me out."

Can you accept the idea that adding 500 yards to the length of a golf course will probably add a few strokes to its difficulty? Can you accept the concept that playing your third round of the day might also add a few strokes to your score? Accept playing in weather with the same degree of common sense. The weather will cause you to score higher (usually) and with more effort and fatigue. Weather is a mental hazard because your reaction to it makes most of the difference in its effects on your game. You don't have to like the weather so much as you must consider it part of the game and make sure you adjust as well as you can. The secret of the mental game, if there is one, is keeping things in perspective.

DISTRACTIONS

Y ou have just lined up your putt. It is fifteen feet uphill and breaks about six inches left to right. You stand over the ball, get set and....

Scenario Number One

Bang! Behind you, a player drops his bag with a crash on the cart path.

105

Scenario Number Two

Bang! Behind you, a tree collapses onto a cart, slightly injuring its two occupants.

Scenario Number Three

You are not sure of the line, so you step back and take another look.

These are all distractions. Of these three scenarios, which one would be most upsetting to your golf game? Number three probably would not be much of a problem at all, especially if taking another look added to your confidence. Number two would not affect your game much, once you went over to help out the folks and found out that they were okay. Number one might irritate you for the rest of the round. How come?

I love it when you know the answer. Of course, the difference is perspective. You are in control of sensing the line of the putt. If you lose it, it is an acceptable distraction to stop your putting routine to reassess what it is you want to do. As for the tree falling, after helping out those poor folks in the cart, you realize how little significance your putt has. Once you have overcome your miniature fight-or-flight response, which was stimulated by the accident, you are ready to positively stroke the ball into the hole.

But! It is not acceptable to have guys throwing their bags down mindlessly while you are trying to play your best. **There was no reason** for that fool to do that and mess you up. Now isn't that interesting! If a distraction has some meaning or reason, it is not a bothersome distraction. Only distractions that are without reasons acceptable to you are really distractions. The mind tends to make up a reason for something's happening if there isn't a clear cause, often to our detriment. For example, that unexpected noise might be taken as a deliberate act, with us as a victim. This could either motivate you or destroy your concentration, depending on your perspective of the event.

What if that fellow throwing down his bag was playing behind you and again did something distracting a little later on? Do

106

you think the second time would be more of a distraction than the first? How come? What if the guy turned out to have some sort of physical handicap that caused the two disturbances? Would that make a difference in your reaction? Would you mentally prepare yourself differently for the remainder of the round?

Remember—what is most important is not what happens, but your reaction and how you cope with your reaction.

SLUMPS

Slumps do not exist. A slump, by definition, is when you are playing worse than you normally do for no logical reason. The justification for classifying slumps as an environmental, and thus a non-existent, hazard is as follows: If you are in a slump, I can think of only three reasons for your suffering and each one means that you're not in a slump. First, you may have some sort of physical or mental problem that is affecting your game. This means the problem is eventually definable if you look hard enough. When you find the problem you will no longer be in a slump. You will simply have a physical or mental problem you need to fix. The second reason you could find yourself in a slump is that you are the victim of an extended period of bad luck. If this is the case, you are not in a slump. You are either being punished by the Golf Gods for some wrongdoing or you have a bad attitude about luck. In either case, you have an identifiable problem and thus are still not in a slump.

The remaining reason you could be in a slump is statistics. If you play golf enough to be interested in reading a book like this, you obviously have played enough to notice that there are times when you play well and times when you don't play so well. Over a long period of time, your scores will fluctuate around your average, some higher, some lower. It's like tossing a coin. Even though there is a fifty-fifty chance the coin will come up heads, you cannot expect the toss to alternate each time—heads, then tails.

Slumps are exactly the same. You can expect hot rounds to occur and "slumps" to occur because of a statistically normal event called the "law of large numbers." For coin tosses this means that you can expect strings of consecutive heads or tails over the long run. Maybe eight heads in a row, sometimes, and even nine or ten

107

tails in a row. When all the tosses are added up, you will still have about half heads and half tails, just what you would expect for a fifty-fifty chance situation. For golf scores, this concept tells you that sometimes your game will not produce scores near your average. This situation can go on for a few games and is normal and to be expected (not necessarily enjoyed). Or you can prolong it if you get frustrated, or decide that you must be doing something wrong and try to fix it. Unless you know there is a physical or a mental problem, or if you know you have offended the Golf Gods, do not fix a slump. It ain't broke.

PHYSICAL HAZARDS

U p until now, I wanted you to assume that even though the environmental hazards are influential, the real hazard is a negative attitude. Physical hazards are similar, but more difficult to overcome. Like almost everything in the mental game, these hazards are not strictly one thing or another but a blend of different elements of our lives. I want to talk about fatigue/injury, fear/tension and burnout as physical hazards. All could have been put into either the emotional or cognitive sections just as easily. I am presenting them here to remind you how tricky it is to define these concepts.

FATIGUE AND INJURY

I read somewhere that a person can perform reasonably well over a long period of time with only four hours of sleep a night. Nothing works normally, I would imagine, but the brain and body seem to be able to adjust. Ken Venturi won a U.S. Open over thirty-six holes sapped of every ounce of physical energy, with his mind turning to watery mush. Probably many other dedicated professionals have done something similar. The hazard of fatigue arises out of our perception of its effects and from trying to overcome our limitations. "I can't go on," is what our body is telling our brain. Don't believe it.

"Watch out for anybody who is sick this week" is a common statement on the pro tours. You do not need to be at your most fit or energized to play your best golf. What you need is coordination among your parts. You do not overcome fatigue; you first endure it

108

and then swing your best, not hardest. Concentration is one of the early casualties of fatigue, your swing one of the last. So if you are overtired, coming down the stretch, wanting to play it out, focus on decision-making first and foremost. Your swing will take care of itself. When I'm very tired, I usually do not drop down one club; instead I make sure I focus on finishing my swing. Pick out a swing cue, like finishing your backswing, and make sure you do that.

Recovering from an injury is more difficult than recovering from the Devil's A*****e pot bunker at Pine Valley. Injuries do a number of things. They hurt. They damage. They keep you from practicing or playing. They change your swing. They are annoying. They are discouraging. They can be scary, expensive and time-consuming. Outside of this, injuries generate two kinds of mentally hazardous reactions: paying too much attention to the injury, or paying too little.

Paying too much attention actually is paying nonproductive attention. Any injury requires an expert appraisal of damage and treatment. If this is not done, doubt about the significance of the injury can cause more difficulty mentally than physically. An injury also gets extra attention if it can be employed as a rationalization for poor play or extra strokes during first-tee wagering. As we discussed before, if you start to believe an injury is a problem, it will certainly become one.

Denying an injury is usually worse than overemphasizing it. Tour players often try to play through a physical problem hoping that the injury is minor and will soon go away. Sometimes this exacerbates the problem and the player is forced to seek major medical intervention when earlier rest might have been the cure.

More players today, though, are aware of fitness and health issues and do not make this mistake. One thing that many players at all levels still tend to do is come back from an injury much too soon. A pro wants to keep his level of play strong and his income high, while the recreational player simply misses the game too much to stay away. Many times, frustration prompts otherwise intelligent people to return before the injury is healed. For others, the cause is pride. "I will show these people that I can get back sooner than they think!" Returning too soon can be avoided if the player has confidence in his physician, understands the rehabilitation process, has set appropriate goals for his recovery and can measure good progress in reaching those goals.

BURNOUT

Worse than fatigue is chronic fatigue, or what is called burnout. Burnout is mental fatigue brought about when the golfer no longer can experience a reward for playing. One of the symptoms of a clinical depression is something called "anhedonia." This is the loss of ability to derive pleasure or enjoyment from doing things. Burnout is a mild case of this kind of depression. The golfer no longer can enjoy or derive any kind of pleasure from his play.

Burnout is not caused by playing too much, in the sense that playing thirty-five tournaments a year is too much, or that playing every day is overdoing it. The problem occurs when the golfer does not get enough reward for his efforts over a period of time. The amount of reward and the span of time are completely individual **perceptions** of what is acceptable. Hungry young tour players could play for many weeks in a row if they were making cuts and stuffing money under the mattress. Retirees can play daily for years, enjoying only old Fred and his terrible jokes and playing mediocre golf, and never feel burnout.

In a way, burnout is like losing patience in slow motion. You are not getting what you want when you want to get it. With impatience, you want it now. With burnout you're not exactly sure what is going on but you know you're missing something. The solution is relatively simple: Either rest, away from golf or serious golf for a time (the amount of time varies), or reset your goals. By creating more immediate goals, those that you can meet easier and sooner, you can rekindle enthusiasm for a while. Eventually with burnout, rest away from the game is the only cure. There are a couple of snags, though, to keep in mind.

For some players, burnout is due to competitive fatigue. The brain can no longer fight without taking a break. For this kind of burnout, rest is best. However, for some people, it is the game that has become a chore, not the fight. Changing for a time to other competitive endeavors will keep the player from going stir crazy at home and returning to the game too soon. Returning before fully rested obviously hastens the return of burnout.

Prevention is the key. By knowing personal needs and style, the mentally knowledgeable can plan ahead, to balance stress time and relaxation time to maximum advantage. The mental game

110

places an emphasis on awareness. Be aware of when to avoid stress completely and when to balance competition and relaxation. This is an individual perception. Some players can be workhorses, while others cannot. There is no one right way. Try hard and long, but do not try too hard and too long. Even practice can be overdone and promote burnout. Too much of anything, no matter how good, is destructive.

FEAR AND TENSION

This hazard is included here because fear is caused by external situations and tension is felt by the body. We all know how easily a lighting-fast ten-foot putt can put fear in our hearts and spasms in our wrists. We cannot pretend to be unafraid, nor can we wish our muscles to relax. This environmental hazard appears at some time in most rounds and all the time for someone with the shanks or the yips.

You can do one or both of two things: You can learn to play with tension, as most pros learn to do, or, you can learn how to turn off muscle tension. Trying something new to overcome fear or tension works for a time because it gives the player a novel situation that distracts for a while and creates hope. But, finding a new club or stroke or a new-style putter usually does not work over the long haul. As soon as tension returns, the so-called solution is lost. Better to solve it than cover it up.

THE EMOTIONAL HAZARDS

Our temperament and what we have learned to perceive create our unique set of emotional hazards. For some of us, emotional hazards are neither deep-seated nor difficult. For others, however, a sweet swing rarely survives the front nine. In competition it is sometimes encouraging to observe another player overreact since it means one less player to beat. That player is busy falling into a mental bunker of his own making. We all know players for whom this is a regular occurrence, and we are astonished at their lack of sense. For others, emotional hazards are so repetitive and destructive that it is sad to watch a wonderful swing fall victim again and again. Although there are as many emotional hazards as there are emotions, I will present only five here.

LOVE

I almost put this emotion in with environmental hazards, since it can be viewed as an outside distraction. Love, like the other emotional hazards, can be ruinous to a good game, or, when understood and put in perspective, become a driving force to better play. From Adam in the Garden of Eden to Wodehouse and *The Heart of a Goof*, affairs of the heart have been the cause of all sorts of trouble.

You have all heard of tour players never fully reaching their potential because they spent too much time enjoying the evening delights of the tour. Until they got married and became responsible, that is. And the opposite is true. Many good players lose interest in the demands of professional life when the spouse waits at home, and very little on the tour can beat the wide-eyed smile of a son or daughter. Balancing the demands of good golf and the expectations of intimacy is difficult, but most easily done from knowing what is really of value. The best players learn that golf is important but not significant, and give golf only the attention it deserves, for short periods of time.

ANXIETY

Certainly more obvious a hazard than love is the anxiety we all experience. Anxiety is distinct from fear because it does not have an external cause, like an attacking bear or a difficult and important golf shot. The cause it does have is ourselves, our ego and sense of dignity and control. The critical audience in our heads can create anxiety. The underlying cause of anxiety is the brain saying, "I don't know what to do, but I know I must do something to prevent a disastrously bad thing from happening to me." The disaster, of course, is losing self esteem, and if we cannot figure out the solution, we continue to lose more and more of the self-esteem we are trying to save.

Another way of understanding this is realizing that the brain knows there is a problem, a very important problem, and is busy looking for a solution. The difficulty is that there is no real problem and, thus, the fruitless search for a solution only stimulates more anxiety. This, in turn, results in more and more missed five-footers, a move to the long putter and finally retirement. The cure is to remove the ego from the golf shot and to tone down the fight-or-flight response.

FRUSTRATION

You already know the formula F = E - R (frustration is the difference between what we want and what we get). However, frustration is more complicated than expecting to make a shot and then merely missing. Missing a shot is best described as disappointment. Disappointment elicits the response, "Darn it. I was hoping to make that." Messing up a shot is experienced differently. As a mental hazard, frustration occurs when the player feels unfairly blocked from achieving a goal, either by himself or by an outside power. Frustration is expressed as, "How could this happen to me?!?!!," and not without a little tinge of anger and a bit of hostility. The difference between frustration and disappointment is that frustration is a blow to the ego.

Earlier, with Nick's reaction, we looked at how a player could miss a short putt because he was more interested in a mental goal than the golf goal. Frustration is one of the major hazards that fuels emotional discharge instead of a smooth golf swing. The player defines the situation as one in which he has tried his hardest and for which he has paid his dues. It is only fair that the result is what he expects. It is an insult, a slap in the face, for the outcome to be anything but good. This is the attitude that promotes frustration.

Once frustrated, the player becomes more easily insulted and the frustration response escalates. All disruptions are a personal affront. Nothing is going right. "Why am I playing this stupid game, anyway?" The player is focused on ego and not golf.

113

CONFIDENCE

If hope is peeking through your fingers and doubt is looking for an exit, then confidence is jumping off a high dive with your eyes wide open while wearing a parachute. Confidence is a blending of expecting success while being fully prepared to face failure. It is not foolhardy chance-taking. It is not necessarily feeling that you will win. It is knowing that you are ready, willing and able to do your best. It is also knowing that your best should be good enough.

Lack of confidence suggests inappropriate goal-setting which has led to a sense of failure. Goals that are set too high, are too far in the future or are not under the player's control easily lead to a crisis in confidence. It can arise from ego frustrations when the golfer has endured too many "unfair" blows. Sometimes it is due to inexperience and fear of the unknown. Whatever the cause, confidence is necessary for choosing the correct shot and finishing the swing. Lack of confidence creates a feeling that something extraordinary is necessary for success, like pulling off a fantastic shot, or getting lucky. Like overcoming frustration, rebuilding confidence requires enjoying positive experiences that tell the player he is back in control. You cannot convince yourself that you are no longer frustrated, nor can you pretend to have confidence. Setting up experiences that create the feeling is the only way up and out.

AROUSAL

If the weather is too bad, if the course is too tough, if the cost is too high or the stakes too low, we don't even bother to put on our spikes. According to one motivational theory, everything we do has an optimal level of arousal for best performance. If we are too excited or don't care, our performance will suffer. Further, this concept suggests that performance on easy tasks will improve with higher arousal, while complicated tasks can be done better with less intensity. As shots differ in difficulty, they also differ in how they add to or detract from our level of intensity.

A half-wedge over water is both more difficult and more scary than a full wedge to an unprotected green. Your arousal for the half-shot will be higher because you are a little worried and because it is a difficult shot. The arousal concept says that you may miss the shot because you are too aroused to play it. Golfers out for a "hit and giggle" round may play very well because they are not overly aroused or play very poorly because they are not trying hard enough.

Good players take into account this arousal idea and use it to advantage. Common on the tour are comments like, "I was pumped up so I took less club." Unfortunately, other statements, such as, "I couldn't feel the fire in my belly" or "I couldn't get up for it," indicate when arousal is low. Arousal is a function of goals, confidence, burnout, ego and a host of other factors. Usually arousal is higher than optimal for most situations and should be lowered by using various relaxation techniques.

CHOKING

W hat a terrible word. No one likes the term and most of us avoid using it. Choking occurs when you are under pressure, a high arousal state, and you are paying more attention to your tension than to your game. The game, your efforts and your response to pressure are all under intense scrutiny but too much is focused on the swirling butterflies in your belly. You feel unable to pull the club back, completely inadequate to hit the ball to the target. Breathing requires all of your attention. Golfers are particularly susceptible to choking because of the free time available to think of the importance of a shot and all of its consequences.

Choking stimulates the fight-or-flight response and puts our self-esteem at risk. Not a very comfortable situation. The answer to choking is both physical and mental, with emphasis about equal between them. You first must diminish the anxiety response with relaxation techniques. As you sense yourself becoming a bit more under control, you then begin positive self-talk and setting of immediate goals, like feeling the club and sensing the finish of the backswing. If you are sensitive to choking, you are not condemned to a tight collar for the remainder of your playing days. The mental game is designed to take such a problem and turn it into productive intensity. Bob Jones could do it at the highest level, and you can do it at yours.

COGNITIVE HAZARDS

As I recall the story, a young René Descartes was once asked during a competition if he inhaled or exhaled at the top of his backswing. He never again picked up a club, thus ending a promising amateur career. He was an early victim of "paralysis by analysis." The cognitive hazards are those constructed by our thought process, which you now know to be faulty at times.

The mind can be looking the wrong way; it can slip, become depressed, make a mistake, be confused, be overloaded or act like a brick. Isn't the game a little more tolerable—when you think about it—knowing that you, as a normal human being, have a brain that sometimes quits on you, a brain that despite your best efforts will not let you perform up to standard? Knowing that no one's mind is a perfect processor of information may allow you to take a little ego out of your game.

CONCENTRATION

Has anyone ever asked you how much you should concentrate on a shot? "I choked down a bit on my brain and played a knockdown concentration." What is "full attention" anyway? Understanding the mental game is realizing that the mind dances from subject to subject often without our control. For us to be successful, the mind must somehow land at the right place at the right time. If you try to move it somewhere, you end up keeping it in the same place. If I nastily told you to ignore the out-of-bounds on the left, your attention would be immediately directed to it. This is the same as telling yourself, "Don't hit it fat." If you want to push your thinking away from an idea, it seems as if you must brace your feet against it, thus drawing attention to what you wanted to avoid in the first place.

Concentration must change its scope and subject, and also its intensity during a golf round. It can be worn out. It can be out of shape. It can be very good, but focused on the wrong thing. I am going to remind you of what you already know:

116

$$\left[\begin{array}{c} \textbf{Concentration is not a thinking activity.} \\ \textbf{It is the result of an action or feeling.} \end{array} \right]$$

Concentration has small ears, except when it comes to negative thoughts. Any time you have some doubt, it seems the mind morbidly rushes over to take a look, like rubberneckers driving by a roadside accident. This is probably because doubt carries extra emotion with it. Another difficulty for concentration is that your mind really believes it can entertain two thoughts at once and get away with it. What do you think happens when part of your mind would like to play a bump-and-run, while another part of you wants to fly the ball to the hole?

MOMENTUM

Avalanches have momentum. So do very large ships. Golfers do not. Momentum does not exist, but let's talk about it anyway. This is another one I almost classify as an environmental hazard since it is something that appears to happen externally to a player. What a hopeless feeling it is when the tide turns against you. You can be five up with six to go and lose momentum. Rarely does being on a roll seem as strong and long lasting as that sinking feeling when momentum turns away. What is momentum anyway? Like so much of the mental game, it is part of your belief system. We tend to believe that luck or momentum is like inertia; things (luck and momentum) tend to keep moving once they start, and tend to be stuck once they stop. If you lose momentum, you think that either you will not get it back or the other guy will find it and keep it.

None of this is true unless you decide to make it true. If you think that momentum is yours, it is. If you think you have lost it, you have. I'd like to propose to you how to redefine momentum so you can use it to your advantage. When you have momentum it is because you are in the flow. You have harmonized all your brains to seek one goal. You have allowed your swing to be at its best. You and you alone are doing it right. **You have created momentum**. Momentum does not happen to you; you make it happen.

117

On the other hand, when momentum appears to be against you, you need to recognize what is really happening. You are a victim of your own negative thinking, nothing more.

Remember the section on ego defense mechanisms? That's when the mind finds excuses for failures so that self-esteem is protected. When you sense momentum change, the defenses may jump in to save the faltering ego. Beware that your focus on momentum may be your ego looking for an out when the going is getting tough. When you think momentum is going against you, focus on the only part of the situation that you can control: your own response. Focus on the things you have control over, like your thought process, relaxation and swing plane.

Now that I have said that momentum doesn't exist, I must admit that it can exist after a stop in play, like a rain delay during a round. A player can become stiff or begin to think about how well he is playing. Negative thoughts can intrude, thus breaking up his focus on the competition. When this happens, your first order of business is to recognize the problem. Once you have identified that you're worried about momentum, congratulate yourself on your awareness and begin devising a solution strategy. Never define the problem as momentum. It is only a change, like wind direction. It is not something ominous. If you identify what has changed and plan the appropriate response, momentum will continue to be a figment of someone else's imagination.

During competition, you may notice when the other player feels he has momentum. Weak-minded players fear this situation, thinking that the opponent will now play with superhuman ability and that luck will be on his side. You keep to the technique of focusing on what you can control and when he eventually loses what he thinks is momentum, you've got him. If he doesn't lose momentum, nothing you could do would have stopped him anyway.

NEGATIVE THOUGHTS

Now seems a good time to talk about negative thinking. Some players are lucky and don't appear to have the kind of minds that do this sort of thing, but most of us do. Basically, negative thinking is the thought that "I can't do this" or "This is not going to work." The problem is that often we are right. Sometimes, what we want to do

118

has less than a fifty-percent chance of success and our negative thinking is accurate. Other times, we think that we will not perform well enough because in our heart of hearts we know our current level of play does not deserve the success we are striving for. These are two very strong stimuli for negative thinking.

What I would like you to recall is that the mind believes what it thinks is true and is better off doing so. (Remember the fiction and nonfiction books?) If you have negative thoughts, **do not ignore them**. A negative thought gives you valuable information. "I am going to hook out of bounds" is a negative thought, yes indeed. It is also what one of your minibrains believes is true. Maybe you really were going to hit out of bounds. Many of your miniminds monitor what your body is doing and how it can perform. If you pretend that this kind of activity doesn't exist, you will end up hitting a compromise shot among various mental intentions. Accept the negative thought as an **accurate mental assessment**. Take it into account and you will improve your mental harmony and gain confidence from your awareness of doing so.

An example of this is when a club doesn't feel right. I have looked at a 150-yard level shot to the green with no wind and from a good lie knowing that it should be a 7-iron for me. But it "feels" like an 8. The negative thought is: a 7-iron is the wrong club. My logic tells me it is the right club for the distance. If I don't trust my feelings at all, I'll hit the 7. If I trust them only enough to choose the 8, but not enough to swing normally, I'll swing extra-hard, believing that it is not enough club. However, if I listen to my negative thought and trust my "senses" I'll swing a smooth 8 and put it within six feet of the flagstick.

MIND-SET

Like an elephant trying to fly, the mind appears to flit about all the options before landing on the one where it was in the first place. Once your mind is made up, which is something that happens very quickly, it ain't going to change in a hundred years. This is true of your liking a course, a tournament, a shot or whatever. What the mind wants to be true it makes true. This is your TV brain (the one that selectively edits what is important) at work. I often counsel golfers that if they don't want to do something, forcing themselves

119

to do so will usually result in increased frustration and further reason for the negative attitude. When we have to do something, our motivation is much lower than if we want to do something.

The answer to handling a mind-set, if you have to change it, is to create *want to*s as well as you can. For example, say you had a negative attitude about a course because of a bad experience when you played it before. If you recognize that you have a mind-set against it, define your negative thoughts as well as you can. Perhaps poor scores on the back nine were the cause of your negative mind-set. You then establish some goals for the back nine that you *want to* reach. Set goals that will give you the feeling of being in control and enjoying yourself. The key is to have you in charge, rather than your mind-set.

OVERLOAD

I want to finish this section on hazards with "overload" because many of you may be experiencing this at times as you go through this book. Overload is obvious; you have more to do or to think about than you can manage to accomplish. This is a little like burnout, a little like underarousal, and a little bit like confidence slipping away. When your mind is overloaded, it tends to reduce the amount of information coming in and processes information more quickly and less accurately. When you feel overloaded, you are. So you better take into account how your mind is becoming saturated. It is not a crime to be overloaded nor is it something to be ashamed of. Unless, of course, you try to pretend that you are okay.

When you feel overloaded, accept this as fact and slow down. Make simple decisions, rely on your caddie or partner and do not overanalyze. Your first decisions will probably be your best. The reason for this is that the mind processes "true" information. Thinking something over means evaluating the relative truths of various possibilities. When your brain is overloaded, it can't do that. So right or wrong, if you are overloaded, you will minimize errors by following the first idea that your mind defines as true. The more effort you make when overloaded, the less chance you have of combining what is really true with what the mind believes is true. It is useless to try to add new information that the overworked mind will think is false anyway.

120

SUMMARY

Mental hazards are simply the golfer's thought processes or assumptions that are counterproductive to a good golf swing. All of them, and I have discussed only a few, are normal, natural, common and sometimes completely unconscious. This makes them difficult to overcome. Part of a complete mental game is to understand your mental hazards as fully as possible and to take steps to reduce their impact. The next chapter presents many solutions that are useful against the mental hazards. Your task will be to match the solutions with your goals and hazards, so that you can have your best game on the course.

11

COGNITIVE
TECHNIQUES

f you have faithfully studied the material so far, you are ready to apply effective techniques to problems you have already identified and those that you will uncover in the future. The end result of applying the techniques is for you to be fully prepared to swing the golf club (or if you are a teacher, to have the student fully prepared). If you understand the concept that the big picture is no picture, I want to further explain how the mental game works to achieve this goal of full preparation.

By assuming that all of the minibrains make up three brains— the thinking, the sensing and the doing brains—it is easy to see that if we are to swing well, the thinking and sensing brains must get out of the way. Since this can't happen, the best we can do is to get the thinking and sensing brains to be thinking and sensing in the right way. This chapter and the next explain techniques to get those two brains organized so as to minimize interference on the doing brain.

ONE SHOT AT A TIME

I fear that everyone but me will tell you to play one shot at a time. I won't tell you to because I don't think it can be done. Physically yes, you can start and end the swing whenever you wish. One swing is easy. Mentally, it is impossible to separate one event from another. Our minds don't work that way.

One player I worked with told me that he wanted his last thought before hitting to be positive. As you know from the brains-talking-all-at-once concept, this can't be done. The brain never rests on one thought, so you cannot delay your hit until you are thinking all positive thoughts. You may have one positive thought or five thousand positive thoughts and fifty-three negative ones, but you cannot wait until you are thinking one positive thought. Your job is to get the flow of all your brains to be as positive as you can.

As you can tell from the three-brains concept, nothing in the mental game is separate from anything else. Remember that the whole brain is always involved.

As you go through the techniques chapters, notice that thinking techniques can be used to reduce tension and that sensing techniques can be useful in focusing the thought process. Being comfortable with the concept that thinking is connected to sensing is connected to doing is connected to thinking is why you have worked hard at understanding the basics. Now you can shine.

GOAL-SETTING

One of the mainstays of sports psychology is good goal-setting. It can cure a lot of ills, from anxiety and burnout to career decisions. As we discussed earlier, there are two elements to good goal-setting:

123

1. Under our control

2. Measurable

To maximize motivational value and to aid in concentration, two other elements for good goal-setting should be added:

3. Interesting (meaningful to the golfer)

4. Reachable (most motivating if there is about a 50% chance of success)

It sounds simple and it is. Let's put goal-setting to work with an LPGA professional. Sumi is a rookie seeking to make her first cut. She has had an exceptional college career and believes that she will win big on the tour. Her fondest dream is to win the Open. Do we define her long-term goal as winning the Open? Some coaches and sports psychologists would say yes, and I can't disagree with them too much. Research suggests that the more specific you make your goal, the better your efforts will be. "Trying hard" is not nearly as good as listing exactly what you want and what you will do.

However, as you know, I like to set goals over which there can be maximum control. So, I would have her define her long-term goal as doing all she can to win the Open. This is how her long-term goal would look for me:

LONG-TERM GOAL

Within five years, to be in a position on the last day to win the Open Championship, as measured by being within striking distance of the lead and having confidence that I can play my best.

Defining the goal this way enables Sumi to focus only on her own game and, in the heat of the battle, know that she is as prepared as possible. Like rungs on a ladder, her short-term goals will provide strong measurable and reinforcing steps toward this far-off goal.

Behind the glamour of tournament week are countless hours

on the range and the putting green. There are lessons to take and disappointments to endure. Concerns and questions about equipment and technique are constant. Short-term goals are vital to overcoming these daily obstacles that can so easily become discouraging. Weekend players know instinctively how to set pleasurable, short-term goals. We would like a good score but are realistic enough to know that often we will be far off the mark. So most of us want only a few good shots in order to declare the round a success. Professionals have it a little tougher.

Short-term goals can be tournament-oriented, like qualifying for the open, or swing-focused, such as becoming comfortable with a new grip. Your job in goal-setting is to design a scheme so that each goal meshes with the others to produce a rewarding step-by-step plan for reaching long-term goals. In a simple plan, this is what it could look like for Sumi:

Tournament Goals

Win Open

Win a Tournament

Contend on last day

Make consecutive cuts

Make a cut

Swing Goals

Know all
the shots

Hit well under
pressure

Hit high long-irons

Hit good long-irons

Be willing to change
old swing habits

125

Mental Goals

Ready to win
major

Value self no
matter what
the result

Belong on the tour

Confidence in the Swing

Confidence I can learn
what I need to know

In listing the goals the way I did, I broke two rules of goal-setting. I did not say how they would be measured, nor are they all the kind that are under the complete control of the player.

That's okay for examples because you know what I mean. What I want *you* to do, however, is to make sure your goal-setting follows as well as possible the four criteria of good goal- setting.

LOGS

Many players compose logs to make sure they are following the goals and methods that have been planned. I've worked with some athletes who list *everything* they do in order to pinpoint exactly what has been of benefit and what may have hurt, including meals and snacks and anything unusual that might have happened on the drive into work. Keeping statistics can help. For example, computing greens in regulation can assist the golfer in identifying a problem area and can also measure progress. These are the kinds of goals that can be set:

1. *Long-term*
    a. *lifetime*   *Known as great player*
    b. *career*   *Win ten Majors*
    c. *ten-year*
       one-year   *Make top ten half the time*
       six-month

2. *Short-term*
    a. *one-month*   *Make top ten three times*
    b. *this tournament*   *Shoot two under for thirty-six holes*
    c. *today*   *Have nine birdie chances*
    d. *this practice*   *Hit ten good shots in a row*
    e. *this hole*   *Keep below the flag*
    f. *this swing*   *Be fully prepared*
3. *Physical*
    a. *swing mechanics*   *Increase shoulder turn*
    b. *strength*   *Leg-lift twenty more pounds*
    c. *flexibility*   *Touch toes*
    d. *health*   *Quit smoking by next month*
4. *Mental*
    a. *mental clubs*   *Improve concentration*
    b. *mental hazards*   *Resolve personal problem*
5. *Etc.*

Practically anything you can measure can be a goal. When you are goal-setting, make sure you take into account mental goals and mental hazards. I have worked with a number of players who have set goals too high because they had unrealistic expectations. For the most part these players had high expectations because it made them feel good. "I'm focusing on making the Tour" made them feel like Tour material. The opposite is also true. A number of players are reluctant to set high enough goals so as to avoid disappointment. Some players limit their potential by playing to avoid bogeys rather than to make birdies, or to avoid three-putting instead of giving the first putt a good chance. Set short- and long-term goals that establish reasonable and motivating steps toward success.

EXPECTATIONS

A kind of mini goal is expectations. The difference between goals and expectations is that we tend to define goals as logical outcomes while expectations, although usually logical, have a bit of emotion to them. As you know, expectations are closely related to frustration and can be a mental hazard. They are also a very important element in insuring success but in a slightly backward fashion. In my mind, goal setting should always be positive and expectations, in some situations, can be very positive if you make them negative.

127

Set your goal to do your best (in some measurable way), then expect Murphy's law to run rampant. Everything that can go wrong will go wrong. Our formula F=E-R can change drastically if our expectations are that things can and will go wrong. It then becomes:

$$F = O - R$$

Which means that if we expect things to go completely wrong and they do, our frustration will be zero or close to it. If we expect things to go wrong and keep sight of our positive goals, no matter what happens, we become positive and motivated. By having at least some negative expectation, like your opponent is going to make that forty-five-foot triple breaking putt to save par, we are better able to handle some of the external and unstable elements of competition, especially in match play. More on this concept a bit later.

MOTIVATION

A person's desire to do something runs from a resentful "have to" all the way to wanting something so much that it can't be done. Setting appropriate goals has a lot to do with creating motivation. A goal such as winning a tournament has both extrinsic and intrinsic motivators attached to it that should be noted. Extrinsic motivation is the pull of external rewards toward the goal, like trophies and prize money. Intrinsic motivation is usually stronger and includes such emotions as satisfaction, pride and joy. Let me show you how this works.

PGA tour players acknowledge that the leading money winner each year is the player who played consistently best all year and in most instances should be recognized as the "Player of the Year." In recent years, winning huge prize money in the season- ending tournament could advance a lower-ranking player into first place. There was a lot of controversy over the large amount of prize money from that one tournament making the full year's play inconsequential. How can professionals, who play for money, possibly complain about *too much* money? The answer is simple. The extrinsic reward of money was displacing the intrinsic value of being player of the year. This certainly documents the considerable power of intrinsic motivation and, at the same time, the significance of losing it.

Intrinsic motivation is based on your value system. Your value system is very strong, very slow to change, and relatively constant from situation to situation. Like most parts of the mental game, you cannot pretend to value something you really don't. The billion-dollar weight-loss industry is founded upon people artificially putting dieting and exercise high on their value list. Within a short time, usually weeks, the willpower evaporates and the person is left with the old fat-producing values back in place. To use the power of intrinsic motivation, you must identify what is important to you and match those values to your game.

Many wealthy people gamble for small stakes, maybe a ten-dollar nassau. Small change, you think, for these guys. What you don't see, though, is the bet made on pride. For these people, this is high-stakes risk, indeed. Losing a few bucks is not the issue; it is the intrinsic motivator, pride, that is at stake. So the way to manage motivation is to set goals according to our four criteria, to identify the extrinsic motivators of your goals and to make sure your goals are those that will enable you to experience emotions high on your intrinsic values list.

THE GAME PLAN

Now let's put together goal-setting, expectations and motivation into a complete package. Whenever you approach the first tee, you always have a game plan. For recreational players it is to enjoy the day, especially with a good shot off the first tee and maybe by having a drink with buddies at the 19th hole. For professionals and tournament players, it is to win or place high, and feel good about their efforts. Did you notice that both groups have two goals as part of their game plans? Game plans should be aimed at achieving both golf goals and mental goals.

A good game plan has two components: a goal or set of goals and a planned response to eventualities. For instance, if you were running a country club, you would establish certain goals like gross income, number of members, expenses, number of rounds per year and other measures of success and growth. You would also try to anticipate problems such as weather damage, inventory problems, cash flow, fungi on the greens and so on. You might buy insurance or otherwise respond to problems and potential problems in a thoughtful, well-planned way.

A game plan for your golf is the same thing. You must establish appropriate goals and devise a contingency plan if what you originally planned for is not happening. The all-or-none player, the one-trial learner who hits a bad shot and decides to mentally quit, has a counterproductive game plan. Once outside his comfort zone, his plan is to give up. We all have a game plan, some of it conscious, like playing for every flagstick, and some of it unconscious, like defending the ego. So let me tell you again: When you think game plan, make sure you also keep thinking mental game too. This means again that there are two game plans, one for your golf and one for your ego.

To play the big course as opposed to the one in your head, you must assess the demands of the course, your particular game and the goal you have identified. Tommy Armour's book, *A Round of Golf*, is a terrific introduction to course management and methods for putting together a game plan. All I want to emphasize for the big-course game plan is for you to think through how you are going to respond to whatever happens, good and bad.

As for the game inside your head, you also must establish goals and a contingency plan. This is one area in which the mental game is easier than the big game. You have predetermined mental goals, self-esteem being the best way to encompass all of them. What you may not have is a plan to cope with threats to your self-esteem and with playing so well that you are outside your comfort zone.

First, you must make sure you keep separate your golf goals and your mental goals. A missed shot, no matter how easy it should have been, is not a threat to your ego. Second, examine how you are defining the problem. Is it bad luck, distractions, other mental hazards? Or is it tough shots, deep bunkers, or other real life external problems? Define the cause of the problem. Third, make sure that you have solutions that protect your ego if your skills (mental and physical) are not up to the task.

As you recall, my efforts at the Tournament of Champions

took into account both my golf and mental goals. I always put together a plan that emphasizes my emotional needs first, then I apply my golf knowledge to improve my play. For example, I set the golf goal of one birdie. When I got that, I implemented my contingency plan, to get another birdie. My mental goal was to enjoy myself. If I had not been having fun from my golf, I would have talked more with Wayne Grady about life on the Tour, or made friends in the gallery or done any number of other things that would have been enjoyable that day. A common game plan on the Tour is to make the cut or be in contention on Sunday. The wise player takes his ego out of the attempt, assumes that Murphy's law is in effect, takes it one shot at a time, as well as that can be done, and reaches his mental goal of knowing that he is fully prepared before each shot and is doing everything possible to reach his golf goals.

Both game plans take a fair amount of effort because they require the player to know his needs and goals and to anticipate problems and create a response to each. If a contingency plan is not made, either one has to be created under the pressure of playing, which often affects play, or the mental goal of reducing tension takes precedence over the golf goals and the player mentally quits. Struggling to save the ego if you do not have a planned response can cause temper tantrums, loss of concentration, tension and a host of other destructive reactions. With a good mental game, we are creating control and methods of reaching our goals; we don't become victims of our primitive reactions.

Below is a simple form that can be used to prepare for tournaments. It includes space for intermediate goals of one to two weeks or so, goals for during play and a simple contingency plan if things go wrong. Note that for each goal there is a column for how to measure success, a list of obstacles and the method or technique for reaching the goal. The examples are for an amateur's first tournament experience.

This type of approach is not for everyone. It is much too organized and logical for some players. All it does is organize what is already going on in your mind. By writing out goals and a game plan you make it easier to know what you want to accomplish and can problem-solve better and retain these ideas better while you are playing. Writing out these things makes them more solid and real. You can even write out how to handle our next topic.

TOURNAMENT PLAN

	GOALS	AS MEASURED BY	OBSTACLES	METHOD
BEFORE	1. short-irons	7 of 10 to target	time	practice
	2. 3-wood	actually doing draw	normally fade	practice
	3. relax	feeling relaxed	new experience	hypnosis imagery
DURING EACH SHOT	1. act relaxed	caddie	tension	breathing
	2. be fully prepared	feeling content	tension	preshot routine

CONTINGENCY PLAN

GOAL	RESPONSE IF FAIL
1. Hit good shot off 1st tee	pick up ball and cheer teammates
2. Par first hole	hit super smooth tee shot on number two

GAMESMANSHIP

Originally, I was going to discuss the comfort zone at this point but then I realized that upon occasion, gamesmanship can knock the best of us out of our game plans and comfort zone. Gamesmanship, of course, is your opponent's deliberately saying or doing something to throw you off balance. For example, jiggling coins in a pocket as you are about to tee off or maybe "accidentally" stepping on the line of your putt are obvious mind games. When things like these happen, you are angry because of your opponent's audacity, then frustrated because you can't do a lot to get back at him. You can. The way to handle gamesmanship is to put back on your opponent the responsibility for his actions and not take on the burden to do something back yourself.

That is, if you try to do something to overcome the effect of your opponent's act of gamesmanship, he has taken your mind off the game and accomplished his purpose. If, however, your game plan includes the following, you will turn the game-playing back on your unethical opponent. Your foe jiggles coins? You tell him that he is distracting you and ask him if he meant to do that. Or, if he walks in your line and you are quite sure it was deliberate, you say, "You walked on my line. Do you need to do that sort of thing to have a chance to win?" The concept is that you point out the actions of your opponent in a neutral way, then ask the kind of question that points out how lame his actions are. If you are a neutral observer of his acts, you'll drive him crazy. If you know you are responding the best way to his gamesmanship, it will improve your play while he takes the responsibility for what he is doing. Keep in mind too, that someone who resorts to gamesmanship is not thinking he can beat you so much as he is thinking he can get you to beat yourself. Prove otherwise. Now, back to applying your mind to your own golf game.

COMFORT ZONE

If all goes well with our game plan, we end up enjoying an experience called the "comfort zone." The comfort zone is both good and bad, like almost everything else in the mental game. (Being in our comfort zone is different from being "in the zone.") Our comfort zone occurs when we are playing our normal game and things are going along pretty much as we expect them to. In important ways, both our golf goals and our mental goals are being met. When you are in your comfort zone, your mind is content because expectations are the same as results (and the results are good). Usually this is measured by score. Partly, it is measured by how we are scoring. If our full shots are superior but our putting is especially poor, even though our score is near normal, we are outside our comfort zone.

The comfort zone is important only when we are playing better than usual or when we want to improve our play. The contentment we feel when in our comfort zone is difficult for the mind to give up. When you are playing very well, it almost appears that this zone requires you to make a few mistakes to get you back to normal. Similarly, when you want to raise your expectations a notch, this feeling of comfort inhibits your efforts to try new shots or set higher goals.

To use your comfort zone to advantage, you must change how you define it. Using your scores, as most amateurs do, either on individual holes or on a complete round, is counterproductive. You are not in charge of your scores and thus your comfort zone is not under your control. Use your game plan to define when you can enjoy the feeling of being in your comfort zone.

A marvelous way of doing this is explained in Kjell Enhager's book, *Quantum Golf*, where he talks about a "quantum scorecard." He suggests scoring the number of "Q swings" in a round as a measure of success. That is, the player counts the number of times he has been able to achieve a "superfluid" swing. The goal of the game plan is to swing this way as much as possible, with little or no focus on the score. You can better control your comfort zone by setting similar goals of relaxed swings, good tempo or whatever best suits your game.

On the professional level it is a little different. Some of the best players in golf approach major tournaments with a target score in mind. They have analyzed the course, the tournament and their abilities to arrive at what they expect to be a winning score. No matter what the rest of the field may be doing, as long as they are at or near their expectations, they are in a comfort zone. Another way of doing this is to set a goal for a unit of play, like three holes or six, and have a target score for this unit. This creates a smaller time span for your comfort zone so that you can more easily adjust to whatever happens.

The danger of the comfort zone is that when you are playing very well, there is a tendency to expect to play worse and you eventually get distracted enough by worrying so that it happens. If, however, you have defined your comfort zone with a reasonable game plan, this will not occur. Your comfort zone will not be so rigid that it cannot accept your improved play.

> **The comfort zone should not be defined by outcome, like scores, but by a process, some action that you can control.**

RITUALS

One thing that we can control is our superstitious behavior and how we make decisions. Competitive golf, no matter at what level, creates anxiety and tension. The difficulty of the game, its inherent unfairness and ever-changing conditions make it a tough task to feel in control. You, as an expert mental player, must figure out how to maximize control. The more you can fulfill all of the elements of your game plan and get into your comfort zone, the better you will play. If these elements are under your control, you have done your job.

Rituals are perfect for some of the elements of your game plan/comfort zone. Like your preshot routine, rituals help you to focus on the game. They also confirm that you are doing what you are supposed to do. Let me give you an example. I worked with an LPGA player who was too nervous to play well and wanted to learn how to relax. One of the cognitive tools we designed was a simple ritual she would do prior to each shot.

Just before she began her preshot routine—in fact it was the first step in her routine—she would have to find a person in the gallery wearing something red. This ritual focused her tension on something other than the competition or her swing and placed it outside of her, yet under her control. Once she spotted something red on someone, she initiated her usual routine. You can imagine her tension if she had trouble finding someone in red and her relief when she did. This kind of tension actually was helpful because it took her mind off her golf anxiety and was the kind of tension she could resolve (simply by finding someone wearing red).

Many players have rituals that begin days before a tournament, like a structured practice schedule or traveling in a certain way. Some rituals are daily, like eating the same breakfast. All of them, no matter how long term or immediate to the swing, should be defined as part of the process of your comfort zone and game plan.

CUING

As with remembering things, it is often a good idea to have a cue word, action or idea to stimulate our thinking or doing. To remember a name, for example, it is helpful to have a descriptive word that will remind us, like the word "wiggly" to remember the name of Dr. Quigley. To begin our preshot routine or to initiate the swing, we can do the same. Sam Snead imagined the feeling of "oily" in order to create a smooth super-powerful swing. Other big hitters like John Daly used the word "kill" to hit the ball off the world. Some use the cue word "now" to start the swing. A forward press or a deep breath can be cues. This method helps to end the thought process and begin the doing.

SELF-TALK

I was once asked how psychotherapy worked. Part of my answer included the phrase ". . . and you talk out loud to someone." We all have conversations in our heads. Often the discussion is: "I'm not sure if a 7-iron is enough. Well it was okay last time. Yeah, but there wasn't quite the same wind. But if I hit it good. . . . Well, I don't know, 'cause on five I hit it a little fat." And so on. I don't know who these different voices are, but as long as they stay inside your mind discussing issues, you will not be as prepared to swing as you ought to be.

The benefit of talk in psychotherapy is that the counselor will make sure the statements are interpreted correctly and used in a positive manner. During competition or whenever the player is anxious about a shot, the self-talk is something like, "I'm not sure I can do well" and other anxious self-doubt thoughts. And as we know, these doubts are translated into poor play. So, by using self-talk techniques, we become our own counselors and create a positive out of a negative. Self-talk is a directed set of statements that you can use to focus positively on the task you want to accomplish.

Take, for example, the experience of most players on the first tee of a tournament. "Oh boy, I'm really nervous," is most often the initial self-talk, accurately identifying what the body is experiencing. Poor self-talk would continue by saying, "I hate being nervous. I wonder if I'm going to screw up. I sure don't want to start off with a hook out of bounds." This creates more tension, and a loss of concentration and sense of control. There are some very useful ways of countering this tendency, all forms of self-talk.

136

POSITIVE THINKING AND TALKING

Positive self-talk does not work if another part of your brain is thinking "I'm a dead duck." The "brains all talking at once" is the culprit for a large portion of missed shots. In order to use self-talk as a tool, **you must accurately and positively respond to all thoughts and feelings.** Being nervous and telling yourself that you are not nervous is ineffective self-talk. Saying to yourself that you are confident when you are outside your comfort zone will not work either. The idea is to give a positive interpretation to whatever you are feeling. And this means *everything*!

Let's go back to the first tee and assume that the butterflies have taken wing. You know that some of that anxiety is due to fearing a bad hit and the subsequent ego bruising. Some is fear of the unknown since this is the first hole, while another portion is simply tension from the situation. All are very valid emotional and physical sensations. Once all of the sensations are identified, self-talk can be used so the player can control his response. Otherwise the mind frantically searches for what would be counterproductive solutions to the negative thoughts and feelings.

Examples of what you could say to yourself on the first tee are the following:

Sensation	Self-Talk
First tee anxiety	*I'm prepared. I have my emotions working for me. I am ready. All I need is to swing smoothly and let my limbic system power the ball long and straight.*

You probably noticed that I used the term "limbic system" in my example of self-talk. I recommend using technical terms like that (as long as they are understood) so as to remind the player of the significant amount of knowledge he has of what is going on inside. Using such phrases works like a cue for a good swing. Being aware of normal yet disruptive responses and knowing that you have the knowledge to monitor and control them adds to a strong belief system and thus to better results. Here's another example.

137

Sensation	Self-Talk
I'm anxious, since I've never played the course well.	*Here we are again. Last time I fell apart on the back nine. I know what I did wrong and will do better this time. I have planned my strategy well. My swing is better and so is my attitude. I am ready to face the challenge.*

Notice that there is no avoidance of recalling the prior bad play on the course. The idea is not to pretend to be positive but to acknowledge the negative so that it can be countered. Identify the problem, not to dwell on it but to fix it. Here's a last example of the concept.

Sensation	Self-Talk
I have not played in months and my swing feels terrible.	*Even though my swing is rusty, I will play my best. I will focus within myself on swinging. I will set enjoyable and reachable goals. I will strive to improve as I play. Whatever I lack in physical smoothness I will make up with mental awareness. I will succeed.*

Getting the picture? Self-talk is reality, not fantasy. Many players automatically do this. By giving themselves a pep talk they unconsciously acknowledge that a problem exists and talk in a positive way about how they are going to overcome the obstacles. You can get very specific. It is usually best to use your own words and phrases unless a coach suggests specific ones.

AFFIRMATIONS

Affirmations are positive statements you make about yourself that add to positive feelings about who you are and what you can accomplish. Like all self-talk, they must be realistic, and to work best, they must be alive with powerful images. Team slogans and fight songs are a form of group affirmations. Here are a few examples of affirmations that golfers may use.

138

A FEW GOLFER'S AFFIRMATIONS

> *I can kill this tee shot.*
>
> *No one can hit this shot like I can.*
>
> *I am the best prepared of anyone.*
>
> *I will play like a tiger today.*
>
> *My grip is strong, my will is strong.*

I think you get the picture. When Gary Player wore all black clothing, this was an affirmation too. He did this to "feel power," so when he dressed, he silently said, "I am powerful." This is both an unspoken affirmation and a bit of a ritual. Both added together to work pretty well during his career.

MENTAL REHEARSAL

At some point before playing, most players are concerned about how well they will perform. For me, prior to a casual round, this will occur about five minutes before tee time. For tour players, this may happen a week prior to a tournament or even earlier. We develop some concern because our anticipating minds are on the alert for upcoming issues and problems. Since our minds are future-oriented toward problems, an effective mental tool is to be future-oriented with self-talk solutions. Mental rehearsal is a good way of doing that.

Although mental rehearsal is primarily a sensing-mind activity, part of it has to do with self-talk, so I will introduce the idea here and explain it more fully in the next chapter. Again, acknowledging the legitimacy of our tension and anxiety is the first order of business. Once this is done, we verbally set goals. "I want to play well. I want to win." Then we rehearse exactly how we will reach the goals. Part of this will be to use self-talk as we rehearse and to use affirmations as we imagine ourselves swinging at the ball.

Mental rehearsal can be very specific, such as imagining yourself on the first tee, or be broad enough to include eating breakfast and driving to the course. The strength of this technique is to instill an "I've been there" feeling and the sense that you will cope with anything that arises and that you will be successful.

The more detailed you can be, the better. The more senses you can experience, the more powerful the rehearsal.

COUNTERING

What happens when you are rehearsing for a tournament in your imagination and all you can do is hit bad shots? Obviously this is not the way to practice success. If negative images and thoughts pop into your consciousness, do not ignore them. I hope that by now you realize that such thoughts are valid and cannot be wished away. As we have discussed, negative thoughts have to be identified, respected and then meaningfully altered into positive statements. Most of the time, negative thinking is the mind's way of protecting the ego so that you do not go out on the course and make a fool of yourself. Countering is the technique that helps you overcome negative thinking by redefining incorrect conclusions. Here is how it works:

Negative Thought: *Oh my gosh! I'm going to hit into the lake.*

Thinking Process: *There is the lake on the right. I have been hitting right. It is highly likely that I will tense up and not hit a good shot. I'm tensing up. I will not hit a good shot. [You know how simple I have made this thought process but this will give you an idea of how the technique works.]*

Countering: *There is the lake on the right. I have been hitting to the right. I am tense and worried about this shot. I am aware of the problem and I have various solutions depending on how worried I am. If I hit an iron off the tee I can take the water out of play. Or, if I swing my 3-wood well, I can also avoid the water. Since I have a number of things I can do, I will pick the one that gives me the most confidence in hitting well and also in having a good chance at par or better.*

This method works by recognizing that your thoughts can accurately define a problem. The difficulty occurs when you begin to worry about the consequences of the problem instead of fixing it.

140

We do this all the time. One bad shot means our swing is terrible. One bad bounce and we are never going to get a break. If we don't play well enough, we don't belong or our friends won't like us, or we are not good for anything. Countering reframes this kind of negative and distorted thinking into constructive problem solving. It is not magic, just good logic.

THOUGHT-STOPPING

One of my favorite techniques for overcoming negative thinking is thought-stopping. It is a combination of self-talk and overloading the senses. The concept is to overwhelm negative thinking and then redirect it. I learned about this method in an unusual way. Picture yourself sitting with your eyes closed as someone suggests to you in a soothing voice to "relax and let go" (as I was doing in reality). The voice softly encourages you to relax your muscles and imagine being on the golf course on a warm summer day. The first tee is beautiful. A gentle breeze is at your back. You are fully relaxed. Then the voice tells you that a slight negative thought has entered your mind. You begin to fear hitting a bad shot. The voice tells you to pay attention to this thought. You might hit the ball off the fairway, maybe even out of bounds.

Unbeknownst to you, the source of this soft voice, this relaxing, soothing presence, has moved behind you as you are thinking this minor negative thought. "STTOOOOOOPPPPPPP!!!!" He yells in your ear. If you're like me, you do stop the negative thinking and jump out of your chair. "Now," he says quickly, "we're going to do this again, only this time, when I yell 'Stop' I want you to imagine a huge blood-red stop sign smashing to within inches of your nose." That was my considerably effective introduction to the technique of thought-stopping.

As I said, the idea is to overpower the negative thinking. Yelling inside your mind helps to do this. Imagining a blood red stop sign adds the power of a visual image to the technique. After yelling at yourself to stop, you refocus your mind on the goal and your plan to reach it. Make sure you yell to yourself, inside your head. This method works by both distracting you from the negative thought and by reasserting your confidence that you have a method that works. I don't think yelling out loud at yourself has the same effect. Doing that seems to increase tension and actually dilutes your mental focus.

SUMMARY

Y ou now know some of the basic cognitive techniques to improve your mental game. I emphasize "basic." Although there is nothing magic about cognitive issues and techniques, they are extraordinarily complicated. One problem is that they can work against you if they are not applied properly. Thought-stopping, for example, can increase your arousal beyond what is best and thus inhibit your performance. Reframing negative thoughts can distract your mind so much that you forget to analyze the golf shot in front of you.

Another problem lies in knowing when to apply a technique, which one to apply and what to do if it doesn't work. Most of the methods we have talked about so far can be applied to any number of situations. An encouraging aspect of the mental game is that one technique can be the solution to a number of problems. Experience will be your best guide as to what works best for you. Sometimes what worked before will not work later. Do not blame the technique. Your mind can become habituated to a technique, just as the body can be habituated to pain medicine, for example, so that it no longer has an effect. This is normal. All you do is pick another form of the technique or choose one that is similar and apply it with confidence.

The more you can involve many parts of your mind in the same activity, the better the results. In the next chapter we will explore a few of the emotional or sensing techniques of the mental game. As you read about them, I would like you to think about how you might combine what you have already learned in this chapter with these new methods. In addition, think about times in the past when they might have been helpful.

12

SENSING TECHNIQUES

C ognitive methods work because they prevent the normal thought process from causing trouble by employing our thinking brains in a way that keeps them from interfering with the swing. Most of us think too much and do not use the more powerful sensing tools that are at our disposal. Neither correct thinking nor sensing is emphasized enough by today's golfer. We golfers also like to make things happen. Tell us what to do and we will do it. Make us change our grips, widen our stance, swing from the inside or turn the hands over. Tell us what action to take and in the quest for better golf, we'll go for it. If we want to hit the ball farther, we hit it harder. If we want to play better, we try harder.

"Active volition" is the term for making something happen. We make the ball move by swinging at it. There is another way. "Passive volition" occurs when we allow something to take place. This is an important portion of the mental game, a part of the mental game of which most players have little knowledge.

In the questionnaire about tension, we discussed that the muscles of the body can produce a good golf swing only if some muscles are tense and others relaxed. The relaxed muscles "allow" the swing to take place. If all muscles were tense, we'd be at the hospital, not on the tee. This is what your mental game can do, too—allow all your minds to be active when appropriate and silent at other times (as much as this is possible).

I think that the sensing brain is more powerful for golf than the thinking brain because it appears to directly translate a "feel" into action without all the interpretations and errors of the thinking brain. This brain is the collection of minibrains that monitors our muscles and stimulates them into action and reaction, in the real world and in our imaginations too. Some scientific studies suggest that passive imagining of swinging is almost as helpful as actually physically practicing the swing. Although studies are not very clear on how this works or how beneficial it is when compared to real practice, you can use its power easily and directly for your golf game.

Remember how we talked about how the brain can create realistic dreams? This is the power of passive volition. As we explore this area, keep in mind that we are talking about mental functioning, just like thinking, only it arises from a different part of the brain. Since all of your brain is involved in all of your golf, you must be as comfortable with your sensing brain as you are with your thinking brain. Once you know how to put all of your brains to work on the same project, you will know the mental game.

THE PRESHOT ROUTINE

We have mentioned the preshot routine a few times so far but haven't defined what it does or how it works. In Chuck Hogan's wonderful and unique videotape, *Nice Shot*, the preshot routine is defined as the switching mechanism that allows the thinking brain

144

to stop and the doing brain to swing. This is as good a description as I have heard.

As we all know, golf requires a lot of thought and numerous decisions. We determine distance, wind and other external conditions. We evaluate how we feel, including strength, confidence and intensity. We make choices like which club to use, ball direction and intended landing area. At some point we must turn off this thinking and hit the ball. The preshot routine is the ending of the pre-swing process and the beginning of the doing.

In order for the preshot routine to work, each part of the brain has to be finished with its own task before it can allow the doing brain to swing the club. Unfinished business causes tension and indecision. The best way of doing this is to have a check-off system, like an airplane pilot's, so that each item is identified, acted upon in the appropriate way and mentally checked off the list.

There are as many systems to use as there are golfers. It doesn't matter much what system you use, as long as it gets you to the point of being ready to hit the ball. There are two ideas to keep in mind, however. First, the preshot routine should not be so automatic that it is a habit. The reason for this is that if it is too automatic, your mind will not be paying enough attention to the process and can wander into tension-producing thoughts or become distracted by outside stimuli. The second point is that the preshot routine should get you to the instant of hitting the ball so you feel ready to hit the ball, not just having finished doing all of the steps of the routine but funneling your attention to the swing. The concept is never to swing until you know you are fully prepared to do so.

View the *Nice Shot* video, read some golf books and talk to other players to get some ideas of how to construct your personal preshot routine. No matter how you do it, I recommend having a two-part routine. The first part should consist of thoughts and decisions about what you are going to do and how you're going to do it. The second should be preparing your mind and body to swing. Dividing the two should be a physical act that becomes the actual switching mechanism to allow you to swing the club with minimal thinking interference.

Here is my preshot routine as an example: Part One is what Richard Coop described in his highly recommended book *Mind Over Golf* as disciplined concentration, or taking the time to make important decisions. Part Two is flow concentration, in which you

145

feel the swing emerging. The description of my preshot routine is not an endorsement of it in particular. I don't play the Tour.

AN AMATEUR'S PRESHOT ROUTINE

PART ONE

The Thinking and Analyzing Process

From behind the ball, I evaluate such things as distance, wind, how the ball is sitting, the potential landing area, my shot expectations. I recall how I have been hitting and basically identify all the issues I can think of.

I define my goal, such as hitting the front of the green and compare how the conditions will help or hinder me in reaching my goal (that is, I now compare my goal to the obstacles).

I look at the options, then I make a decision on the club and decide how I want the ball to fly and land. I then visualize doing this to see how it feels. If all is well. . . .

I exhale and relax, and walk over an imaginary line about four feet in back of my ball.

No more thinking

PART TWO

Sensing the Shot

I line up the clubface to the target, take my stance, look at the target, waggle the club and reset my feet twice.

146

I look at the target,
look at the ball,
clear my mind,
hit.

Many very good players do not appear to do all these things, but they do. Some rely on years of experience to short-cut many of the things I do step by step. Some use intuition instead of thoughts to make decisions. If you are kinesthetic or visual, for example, you may not need to rely much on yardage markers as the more verbal-brain players do.

Your preshot routine should respond to your assets and liabilities so that you can be fully prepared to hit the ball no matter what the circumstances. Players who are easily distracted should design complicated yet short routines. Players who have a tendency to get anxious often benefit from slower routines that emphasize tension relief and give them time to regain a sense of control.

An awful lot can be accomplished by your routine. Experiment a little to find your best method. At times your routine will become stale. That is normal. All you have to do is alter it a bit and it will function well again. Now we must find out what that point of being ready to swing looks like.

One last idea on the preshot routine. When I say "no more thoughts," what I mean is that you do not have words in your mind any more. We want to be finished and out of the verbal minibrains so that the sensing minibrains can command our full attention.

RELAXATION

A relaxed mind and body are what deliver power to the ball. **Your doing brain will automatically create the tension that is required for hitting the ball if you let it.** This means that your job is to be mentally and physically relaxed at the time you begin the swing. Naturally, you must be able to identify when you are relaxed to the degree that produces the best swing. This is no easy task.

All three "minds" have to be relaxed. The cognitive mind must be finished with the thought process. The sensing mind must be content and not on the lookout for any unresolved conflicts. And

147

the doing mind must be relaxed and ready. You have a good idea already about the thinking mind and how to get it ready. Both the sensing and doing mind can benefit from becoming relaxed.

There has been debate in psychology about anxiety causing muscle tension or muscle tension causing anxiety. No matter. If you know how to relax your muscle tension, and concentrate on techniques to do so, you will relax yourself well enough to swing your best.

There are excellent published methods of relaxing available. Robert Rotella and Linda Bunker's excellent book, *Mind Mastery for Winning Golf*, describes a number of very good ways. I like a version of Edmond Jacobson's "progressive relaxation" that seems to be a simple and effective technique. Let me caution you, though, that without practice, any relaxation technique will have limited value. The profit is both long term and immediate.

The idea is to use the technique to lower your normal level of tension since most of us carry around more daily tension than we need anyway and the less the better. Another benefit is that the more you can sense tension, the better able you will be to know when it is a problem. Last, as you lower your general level of tension, you will play with less, have the ability to spot it creeping into your game and know how to get rid of it when it does.

While playing, you must have the ability to relax for that short period just before and during the swing. Knowing what level of tension is best for your game allows you to monitor your level and adjust yourself as necessary. As I said, having less general tension helps, as does the confidence that you know specific techniques for relaxation when you need them.

When I teach this method, I recommend practicing twice a day for about ten to fifteen minutes and for half a minute or so whenever you think about it. Relaxation tapes are good and help you learn more quickly. My impression, though, is that they tend to make you too dependent on the tape rather than on your own body sense. I think if you learn the method on your own, you will be able to use it better on the course.

HOW TO RELAX

First, find a comfortable upright chair in a quiet room. Do not lie down on a bed. I want you to learn this well enough so you can

148

*relax while standing. Do the relaxing with your eyes closed the
first few times so you can better feel what your body is doing. Later,
practice with your eyes open.*

*Second, after you're sitting comfortably with both feet on the floor
and your hands apart and resting on your lap, focus on your
breathing. Gradually allow it to become slow, smooth and deep. As
well as you can, breathe deeply down in your stomach, not high in
your chest. Breath with this slow, smooth rhythm for two minutes
or so.*

*Next, focus on what your hands feel like. Sense your fingers, palms
and the tops of your hands. As you get a sense of the shape of your
hands and all the small muscles, allow the muscles to relax more
and more each time you exhale. Do this for five or six breathing
cycles. Then sense your forearms and upper arms also becoming
more relaxed. Focus on your arms relaxing for five or six cycles,
too.*

*Repeat this for your feet and legs. Then for all your trunk muscles,
your buttocks, stomach, chest and back. Then do your shoulders.
The shoulders usually carry some extra tension so it often helps if
you move them around a little in order to feel them better before you
begin to relax them. Next comes your neck, then move your jaw
around a little before you relax it. Then your facial muscles (feel
them smooth out). And, last, feel your eye muscles relax.*

*So the units are: hands, forearms and upper arms, feet, calves and
thighs, trunk, shoulders, neck, jaw, face, eyes.*

*You can deepen your relaxation by repeating this procedure.
Instead of just relaxing, what you do is sense a feeling of heaviness
in your limbs, trunk, and head. With each exhalation (again, five or
six), you sense the area feeling heavier.*

If you practice this method, you will soon learn how to relax
deeply in a very short period of time. As you go about your daily
business, you can improve your relaxation abilities by stopping for a
moment and taking stock of your tension. Almost always it will be
higher than necessary. Take that moment to slow your breathing and
with each exhalation allow one of the muscle areas to relax. The one I
almost always choose is the shoulders, which is where most of my

149

tension is stored. Within one or two breathing cycles you will be able to feel the difference. This method transfers very well to the golf course.

MEDITATION

Comparable yet opposite to the relaxation technique I just described is meditation. Jacobson's and similar methods are designed primarily to enable the muscles to relax the mind and to teach the individual the feel of a relaxed body. Meditation relaxes the mind first so that the body can then also relax. Both approaches work very well. As with relaxation techniques, there are many ways of meditation. Books and experts on the subject abound. Basically you need a quiet place, some sort of thought, like a mantra, to focus on and an attitude of "letting go." A mantra is a repeated meaningless, rhythmic sound that helps focus the thinking, sensing and even doing minds.

The idea is to sit (in various ways, depending on the kind of meditating) and let your mind passively attend to the mantra. The meditator learns not to worry about a wandering mind. This passive attitude is one of the important benefits of meditation. Practice is usually twice a day for twenty to thirty minutes.

AUTOGENIC TRAINING

Another popular method involves sensing heaviness and warmth as the vehicle for relaxation. As with the Jacobson technique, you focus on the arms and then the legs. For example, you repeat the statement: "My arm is heavy." Then you do the same for the sensation of warmth: "My arm is warm." Next you say, "My heartbeat is slow and calm." You then focus on repeating, "My breathing is slow and calm." Next, "My stomach is warm." Last, "my forehead is cool."

By saying these words and focusing on the physical sensation, you are defining the perception in your verbal brain and combining it with the physical expression of relaxation. This does wonders for coordinating the sensing and thinking brains. If practiced for five

150

minutes four or five times a day, this method is very powerful for mind/body control. It does take a long time to develop real proficiency under competitive conditions, however.

IMAGERY

Imagery is another powerful tool used by most of the top players. "Seeing" the ball flight in your mind's eye aids the body in sensing what it is about to accomplish. Seeing is believing and believing is doing. Imagery can be of a number of things: the line of a putt, the flight of the ball, the target, the feel of a chip, the sound of a bunker shot or the feeling of accomplishment at the awards ceremony.

As with everything else, however, we all have different abilities in producing the mental image that will be of most help. Some players can imagine the shot from start to finish, even to the point of hearing the ball land a hundred yards away. Others can't see a thing and think that imagery is a waste of time. There are day-to-day changes in ability, too, to take into account.

Imagery is the controlled use of the senses to prepare or program the doing brain. It is like using the power of dreaming in a way that helps us to reach our athletic goals. The theory behind this technique is based on the idea that the mind sends signals to the muscles for them to swing the club. If the mind can imagine the swing in great detail or with the appropriate senses, the same or similar messages are sent to the muscles as in an actual golf swing—mental practice instead of physical practice. As I mentioned before, there is some scientific evidence that this really occurs. Another benefit of imagery is that it adds to the player's sense of "being there." If you have actively imagined putting for the Open title, then when you are actually in that situation you have a little more ammunition to help you make the putt.

Most importantly, imagery seems to effectively and efficiently prepare the doing brain to swing the club.

To use imagery, you must first learn what kind you do best and what you may want to practice and improve. There are as many kinds of imagery as there are senses: seeing, hearing, smelling, tasting, touching and doing (kinesthetic). The more you can use, the more realistic and powerful the image. Visual imaging is usually defined as the easiest to do and also the strongest. Let's take a look at a few examples of its use.

151

VISUAL

A common method of sensing the line of a putt is to imagine a white line from the cup to just past your ball, following the line. If you can "see" this line, all you do is take the putter back on the white line and follow through on the line. This is visualization while you play. Another example of this is to pick a spot in front of your ball to help you find the line to a distant target. A patch of brown grass a foot in front of the ball will help you line up the clubface. You use visual imagery when you sense that patch as the target for your follow-through.

A step removed from using imagery as a swing target is to use it to imagine the flight of the ball. As part of your preshot routine, you might stand behind the ball and "see" the ball sail high and long to the center of the fairway, landing on the spot you have visualized. Sitting on a bench waiting for your turn to hit, you can watch yourself go through your routine and hit the ball to your target. This is often a good idea if you need to improve your concentration, if you are frustrated or distracted or perhaps want to avoid looking at another's swing.

You can use visualization before a match, watching yourself play the entire course, and add self-talk to enrich the sensations. This method is also useful for reviewing your play of yesterday or last week, perhaps noting where errors occurred as you relive the experience. When you get good at this technique, you will be able to sense other occurrences, such as increased tension, that you can then address directly. For example, when I was preparing for the Tournament of Champions, I visualized myself on the first tee. After watching myself a few times, I noticed I wasn't breathing. I added the kinesthetic sense of breathing when I practiced my pre-tournament imagery. Naturally, I took this into account when I readied myself to actually hit the ball. Here is a quick look at other senses.

AUDITORY

I thought I had invented this technique until I heard the same idea from a Canadian professional. For a while I was intimidated when I faced a ball sitting up in a bunker. I feared skulling the ball across the

152

green into another bunker. Imagery is a great way to get out of the thinking brain into the doing. Since I could not visualize a good shot (I am weak at visual imagery), I was stuck until I decided to "hear" the shot. As part of my preshot routine, I imagined what a successful shot out of the sand would sound like and imagined myself hitting the sand so as to produce that sound.

As part of my mental preparation for my moment of glory at La Costa, I also imagined the sounds of the first tee and the quiet as I addressed the ball. Even silence can be an auditory stimulus to imagining or anticipating.

OLFACTORY/TASTE

These are less powerful in aiding the swing or coping with the game but are useful in previewing and preparing for a situation. I set up a ritual for La Costa so I could define myself as fully prepared and thus maximize my feeling of confidence. Part of that ritual was to enjoy a half a cup of coffee. You can see that if this taste was part of my pre-tournament imagery, and if I actually followed my ritual, I was fully preparing myself mentally for the challenge ahead. Preparation for the Masters might include a whiff of dogwood or azalea.

TACTILE

This is a terrific one for golf. The sense of touch on the club is extraordinarily important to good play. Being aware of your grip, the position and feel of the hands, having a sense of power and yet sensitivity is mandatory for having confidence in the swing. Have you thought of sensing more how your feet feel on the teeing ground or in the sand? Using tactile imagery before the shot or in imagining playing a few holes can greatly strengthen the realism of the experience and contribute to stronger mental images.

KINESTHETIC

Perhaps the second-most powerful imaging technique for golf is the sense of body movement. Prior to hitting a chip, most of us

153

swing the club a few times to get the feel of what we want to do. Sensing the putting stroke a few times before a putt is another way of employing the feeling sense. Using imagination to do the same thing works very well. You can imagine the feel of chips, half-swings, full swings or even a slow, relaxed walk to your ball.

HOW TO USE IMAGERY

Imagery must be specific. You must have a clear idea of what you want to imagine and what senses to use. It must be positive, of course. It must be realistic, as well. It is of no use to imagine yourself performing beyond reasonable expectations. Your mind is not stupid and will be insulted and bored if your imagining powers are toyed with. For best results, you should use imagery from an internal perspective and not from the outside. That is, imagine yourself swinging the club, not watching yourself doing the same thing as if you were on television. If you can't do it from inside (some people cannot), then an external view will work well enough.

Visualize or image from a relaxed perspective. When practicing, it is useful to do relaxation techniques first. Some people respond well to guided imagery, a technique in which someone else, a coach, psychologist or perhaps a prerecorded tape tells you what to imagine. I advocate getting the thinking brain involved with cuing or triggering words while imaging. For example, my preparation for my tournament included the word "liquid" just prior to visualizing my swing on the first tee. This enabled me to cue my mind and body to a positive image and feel. Recalling the word liquid on the first tee prepared my body to perform what it had practiced in my head.

TARGET

Our minds need a goal and for most imaging the mental goal is your target. For visual imaging, the target is most often the landing area, green or hole. Sometimes it is the line of the putt or flight of the ball. Whatever it is, you should have a clear image of your visual target.

154

For the other senses, the target is different. Targets are the sound of the club hitting the ball, the taste of coffee, the feeling of success or pronation of the hands. When you use this technique, always have a target sensation in mind. Have some predefined outcome for your imagination to reach.

As with almost everything else, the more you practice the better you will get. Imagery is best practiced at first after a round or after hitting balls. This gives the mind more sensations to draw from in the beginning. After you get some experience, you can create images of what you want to happen in the future. It is a powerful technique that many players happen upon informally and don't exploit to its full potential. Determine what your imaging abilities are and add them to your complete game.

MENTAL PRACTICE

When we talked about mental rehearsal, it was defined as a method of creating a "been there before" mentality and of setting goals and anticipating problems. To benefit further from this technique, we can add the power of mental imagery. Mental practice is using all of the mind's power to create a lifelike situation with your imagination. You can do this while sitting in your easy chair at home imagining you are competing in tomorrow's tournament. From getting up and having breakfast to signing your scorecard, you can mentally produce goals, swings, conversations, contingency plans, walks through the rough, the taste of a peanut butter sandwich at the turn and anything else that helps you experience the situation before you get there.

You can create mental practice while physically practicing as well. Many players put pressure on themselves while practicing in order to prepare for tournament conditions. Don't leave the putting green until you have made ten eight-footers in a row. Practice your swing at a crowded driving range to learn how to tune out distractions. Be creative in setting up various experiences for your senses. However you do this, always have a personally measurable outcome, such as feeling competent, enjoying a sense of satisfaction or seeing the line of a putt better.

155

FUN

In talking with successful athletes, I am struck by how many of them include having fun as a method for doing their best. It would seem that having fun would instill a less serious attitude and lower motivation for reaching a goal, almost like a teenager's approach to washing a car. He would make it fun and the car would not get very clean. Having fun often appears to be an easier and more reachable mental goal than something like satisfaction and thus, having fun distracts from the goal. Casual golf, for example, is rarely good golf.

If you think about it, though, having fun is an attitude rather than a goal for serious players. "Hit and giggle" is the definition of fun for the weekend bring-along-a-couple-of-cases-of-beer-in-the-cooler set. Having fun for the serious player is the competition and the challenge. Having fun is nonjudgmental, too. If you play and have fun you are not busy protecting your ego. Having fun is playing relaxed. Having fun is allowing events to occur, going with the flow and having your expectations equal reality.

When you play, you have certain assumptions of what it takes to play well. Many golfers make the mistake of thinking that a serious approach is the only road to success. For some, it is. These players have a mental par that doing your best is hard work. If this kind of player did not feel like he was working hard, he would feel like he was not trying. For others, a better way to succeed is by approaching the game with a more relaxed attitude. **MAXIMUM EFFORT DOES NOT MEAN THE HARDEST EFFORT**. Just like the best swing is not harder but better, the best mental approach is not more serious but better. You have to determine where on the continuum of tension/relaxation or work/fun lies your best game.

AGGRESSION

No one should play aggressive golf. Most people define aggressive golf as going for a tight pin or hitting driver down a narrow fairway. From now on, define this kind of play as gambling, go-for-it or attacking golf. And from now on, define aggressive golf as the inappropriate expression of frustration, hostility or anger. When a player

156

three-putts a green, goes to the next tee and blasts his driver, he is not playing golf. He is expressing his anger. He is being aggressive. He is not playing a good mental game.

When a player takes a chance by shooting at a pin tucked behind a deep bunker, he may be playing attacking golf or being aggressive, depending on his reasoning and goals. If he is two down with two to play, he is playing attacking golf. If he is angry and frustrated that his opponent has had all the luck and it's about time he enjoyed some, he is being aggressive. Aggression is a mental hazard.

Instead of playing aggressive golf, be assertive. Assertive golf is playing with the attitude that you are doing your best to win, that you want to and deserve to win and that you are going to overcome all obstacles in your path to victory. This approach creates an attitude of doing your best and accepting that someone else may do better. If you get caught up in comparing your present performance against the field or your match play opponent, your negative emotional needs (such as dominance) will become stimulated and you will fall victim to these mental hazards. Your play should not be measured or valued until after the round. You do that by focusing on your assertive play, not by playing aggressive golf.

CONCENTRATION

One last word on concentration is in order. Always remember that concentration is not a thinking activity. Concentration is the focus on doing something, like sensing the finish of the backswing. It has been explained from a number of perspectives, but the one I want you to remember is this one:

$$\left[\textbf{Concentration is the focus on doing or sensing} \right]$$

You cannot concentrate by thinking about it, but you can by focusing on an emotional or physical sensation. All of the sensing techniques we have summarized in this chapter are good methods of improving your concentration.

157

SUMMARY

The best players in the world have either sought help in understanding the sensing brain or were lucky enough to have experimented productively with their innate talents. I don't know of any who can't improve. The difficulty with the sensing mind is the concept of passive volition. This attitude is against all that we know that has worked in the past. If something is not working, we all have been trained to try harder. However, as an example we all know, trying harder to concentrate makes concentration next to impossible.

The thinking brain, the seat of our primary identity and reference point, always wants to be in charge. Athletes often say, "I really want to win so I can't relax and just let my body take control." Yet giving up control is what enables us to play our best. The thinking mind has only the role of analyzing some data, such as distance. The sensing brain then adds more information such as "I feel like I can crush this shot" and adds some of the method for achieving the desired outcome by imaging. The doing brain then must be allowed to contract and relax the muscles as needed. This creates the symphony of mind and body necessary for playing your best.

This chapter has emphasized some of the sensing power of the mind. There is a considerable amount that we have not covered in this short section. How to measure your individual strengths and weaknesses is a book in itself. My intention has been to document in the prior chapters the importance of the mental game and in the latter portion to give you some ideas on its application. If you want to increase the abilities of your sensing mind, you will need to get more information and probably some guided practice.

The concluding chapter will put all that you have learned together so that you will know how to go on from here.

158

||||||

13

GOLF SMART

e have covered a lot of territory investigating the mental game, its hazards, clubs and techniques. Now it's time to put the mental fundamentals into a mental golf bag so that you can carry them with you on any course in the world and under every condition imaginable. Each time you play, you will be using some of what we have discussed. Competitive golfers will most often be facing a tough field or an opponent as tough and consistent as old man par. Recreational players are after an enjoyable way of transferring what they learn to the golf course without a lot of work and effort. This last chapter will address the needs of both groups.

"To thine own self be true," will be our motto as we course through the final concepts and ideas of the mental game. Too many players become confused or misled seeking the secrets of golf. There aren't any. The best players all do what works for them. That does not mean that what made them a success will work for you. None of them, and I repeat, none of them thought they had it all. But what they had, they believed in. In his *Little Red Book* Harvey Penick advised to "be yourself" and to "be at ease." The idea is to learn how to create an internal balance between the demands of golf and belief in yourself.

PLAY YOUR BEST

"Never never never never never never give up," is a popular paraphrase of Sir Winston Churchill's address at the Harrow School during the dark days of 1941.

We all want to play our best. But, what does playing your best really mean? Is maximizing your potential playing your best? If it is, how do you know when you have done it? Is trying your hardest playing your best? We all know of players who might have won a lot more if only they didn't put so much pressure on themselves or try so hard or if they had played smarter or more aggressively or less aggressively. Something should have been different. Did these players reach their potential? If you asked any of these players whether their style of play affected their success, many of them would answer that they may have lost here and there because of their style, but each would insist that "I had to play my own game." I think they played their best because they didn't expand their potential.

> **Potential is not a ceiling, it merely marks where the real work begins.**

Superiority in the mental game is all about overcoming your natural tendencies and limitations.

Does reaching your goals mean you have played your best? It all depends on the kind of goals you have set. If you have set and reached golf goals, you have not played your best. You have succeeded nicely in setting and accomplishing goals. You have probably improved your game. But, maybe your goals did not stretch you to play your best. Can playing your best include making mistakes?

160

Suppose you set a goal of shooting par. On the last hole you miss a two-foot birdie putt that leaves you at one under. You exceeded your goal. Have you played your best?

In a way, playing your best is satisfying your critical audience. We instill a tremendous amount of power in the judgment of these phantom images in our minds. Winning one for Dad, Mom, the coach, the school, the history books or overcoming a label of "choker" or paralyzing anxiety may all describe playing your best.

But if you think about it, meeting the expectations of the critical audience is actually meeting your own need to feel a sense of worth, competence or satisfaction. Playing your best means playing well enough to satisfy your real self.

Competitors think this kind of discussion is stupid. Who cares about all this psychological mumbo jumbo? Playing your best is winning. Nothing else. If you win, you have done your job. Best isn't the idea. It's whatever it takes to win that's important, whether it's with your "A" game or grinding it out. This single-mindedness toward wining is necessary for success, but not in the way these folks think.

Winning in the mental game is not against the course or an opponent, but winning with (not against) yourself. Winning from this viewpoint is reaching golf goals and mental goals with the same method. For example, imagine facing a four-foot putt for a championship. Your golf goal would be to sink the putt while your mental goal would be the enjoyment of victory. A good mental game would emphasize the immediate golf goal of putting a good stroke on the ball and the immediate mental goal of feeling satisfied with that very same effort at a good putting stroke. If you are meeting your mental and golf needs as you play, you are playing the absolute best you can. Playing your best is making mental pars. Make the mental pars and the game will take care of itself. Playing with relaxed intensity and with a nonjugmental attitude will lead you to being in the zone.

PLAY YOUR OWN GAME

PART ONE

My Uncle Bill, a member of the Prestonfield Golf Club in Edinburgh, once told me that he played by "hitting the ball, going to find it, and hitting it again." He would never read a sports psychology book and I doubt that he has ever read a golf instruction book either. Yet, he and his friend Sandy always take the match from me, and I have read all the books. These two canny Scots know their own game.

Playing your own game is not relying on your natural talent, but combining what you have experienced yourself with what you have learned from others. Playing your own game also means understanding how your personality and unique perceptions make you cling to old habits, limit your acceptance of new methods and inhibit your ability to apply them. As we discussed earlier, a good mental game requires a special kind of awareness: the awareness of all your mental pars, mental hazards, and mental clubs.

MENTAL PARS AND COURSE MANAGEMENT

If course management was only a matter of intelligence and experience, all of us with an I.Q. over 80 would be scoring a lot better. Playing good golf, course management, the mental game, playing your best are all the same thing. The game of golf sets up the challenge; your mental processes interpret the challenge so that self-esteem is preserved. The course architect knows about the mental game and uses our weaknesses to strengthen the course. "You can reach this par-five in two; it's easy," he whispers as you look down the fairway. The architect has designed a hole that looks like an easy birdie chance, but is much more difficult than it looks. You're licking your chops. Easy birdie, a chance of eagle. Your golf goal is quickly defined as a four on the card. Now your mental game comes into play as your friend or your enemy. If your mental goal of feeling satisfaction can occur only with birdie or better, the golf course has won.

An attacking player, for example, would define playing safe on this hole as backing off from a good birdie chance. This causes conflict between ego needs and golf logic. Hitting driver off the tee will improve his chances of birdie and make him feel good, but also increases his chances of missing the fairway or landing in a bunker. The attacking player's ego will encourage him to attack. When he attacks the hole, it is the architect and the player's personality making the course-management decision. This is the exact opposite of a good mental game. This kind of decision should be made using golf logic, and not self-esteem. Yet, good golf does not have to be sacrificed to preserve self-esteem.

Maturity as a golfer arrives when the game is played according to golf logic and not ego.

MENTAL PAR AND SELF-MANAGEMENT

T hen again, playing only by logic is no fun. Without heart, tension and risk, golf has no reason to be played. "The good players have always used the anxiety factor in their favor," said Hale Irwin prior to his defense of the U.S. Open Championship, ". . . it manifests itself almost in serenity." This is a great description of how the mental game is applied to course- and self-management. The Japanese call it *Wa*, for circle or harmony. It occurs when the player adjusts to the situation, removes his ego from his efforts and is fully involved in the shot at hand.

Let me talk a little about how this doesn't occur and then look at the positive side. The average 18-handicap player is well aware of his limitations. Faced with a green side-bunker shot, he will invariably tense up, swing hard, and either bury the club in the sand or skull the ball over the green. He knows he's tense, so he swings hard. The golf goal is to get the ball on the green close to the hole, while the player realizes that he has very little chance of doing that. Self-esteem rests on getting the ball out of the sand and onto the green. The usual bad shot reminds the player of his lack of ability and chips away at his ego. Compare this state of mind with the other approach.

"I played my best when I felt I was almost hypnotized," reported Tommy Jacobs during an interview a few years after his retirement from the tour. What he said fits into our idea of achieving mental pars. The swing is smooth, strong and powerful. It is not quick and it is not forced. The golf course is not an enemy to be defeated, but more of a canvas on which we can perform our art. What Tommy described as "hypnotized" is harmony within the self.

In more concrete terms, this harmony is achieved when the player's ego is not at risk, when the player is enjoying the process of playing, when his golf goals match his emotional needs and when he plays with relaxed intensity.

Our 18-handicapper in the bunker would do well to change

his golf goal from putting the ball on the green, which is way out of his control, to remembering one sand technique he read about and trying to do that. If the player focuses on what he can do, he will be much more likely to do it. This takes away the worry about where the ball will go, relaxes his muscles so that he will swing more comfortably, feel better and achieve golf and mental success. Harmony with golf and self.

Only you know what this feels like for you. Your job for the mental game is to define what creates internal harmony, to identify what this feels like and to construct methods of getting there. For example, one of the ways I encourage players to achieve the mental par of satisfaction is to define it as being fully prepared for each shot. This goal fulfils all the criteria of goal-setting and meets ego and golf needs at the same time.

All that we have discussed so far about the brain and mind converges here, with your individual sense of what is right; what makes you feel good and produces good golf. This feeling, unfortunately, often changes. Our abilities change and our challenges change, too. But that really doesn't matter. For example, the competitive golfer needs to feel competitive fire. Some days it just isn't there. It can be artificially created for a time by short-term goals and challenges. But somewhere inside, that competitive minibrain is on vacation. Let it rest. Just don't be too surprised or upset if the search for your inner sense of relaxed intensity and a nonjudgmental attitude isn't always easy. Also, don't get discouraged if it is hard. Your goal should be to capture this feeling as often as you can. The harder you look for it, the more elusive it will be. The more you try to evaluate and control all your minibrains, the less you are allowing them to do their jobs. Look for internal harmony gently but with diligence. Be aware of how you feel and use your mental techniques to shape your goals and the ways you reach them.

PLAY YOUR OWN GAME

FINAL PART

There are many things we have not talked about. We could have looked more at teaching and learning, or how to handle specific situations like match play and the psychological differences between

164

putting and full shots. One difference is that an error with a full power shot is easier for the ego to accept than one that requires just a "touch." We did not talk about team play at all. Since there are many very good books available that can add more arrows to your quiver, I will not duplicate their efforts here. Our task was to explore the basics of your mental game.

We began by talking about the mental game as a belief system, yours in particular, and that is where we will finish. Self-belief is the basis of a good mental game. You do not have to believe that your swing is the best it can be. That's too much of a focus on the physical game. The belief I'm talking about is that each of your three brains can do the job. Pay attention to all of your minds. Do not make the mistake of pretending all is well if it isn't. Listen to your fears and you will no longer have them. Sense your tension so you can become relaxed. Acknowledge your negative thoughts so you can be positive. Your body can perform only what the mind allows it to do.

Your job is to take the power of your mind seriously. All the successful players do. For your best game, look inside your mind: your perceptions, perspective, thinking, feelings, your defenses, expectations—everything we have talked about. However, don't feel that you must figure all this out by yourself. The physical game can be learned on your own because the flight of the ball is proof of your swing. Often your mental game is best reflected by someone else—a teacher, coach or sports psychologist. Books on the mental game offer a lot of advice. One I recommend to all players for improving perspective is Ken Blanchard's *Playing the Great Game of Golf*. Now, I think you are ready to decide what is best for you. Listen to others and make up your own mind.

I hope that now you have a good idea of what your own game is and how to find it. Good luck.

BIBLIOGRAPHY

Armour, Tommy. *A Round of Golf with Tommy Armour*. New York: Lyons & Burford, Publishers, 1993.

Bensen, D. R.(ed.). *Fore! The Best of Wodehouse on Golf*. New York: Ticknor and Fields, 1983.

Blanchard, Ken. *Playing the Great Game of Golf*. New York: William Morrow, 1992.

Blanchard, Kenneth, and Bob Toski. "The One Minute Golfer," New York: *Golf Digest*, June 1985, pp. 53-60.

Bonar, A. J., James Schwartz, and Bob Brown. "Would You Like a Mulligan?" [videotape]. San Diego: San Diego Golf Academy, 1991.

Brown, Bob. *A Thousand Rounds of Golf*, San Diego: San Diego Golf Academy, 1990.

Cochran, A. J. (ed.). *Science and Golf*. London: E. and F.N. Spon, 1990.

Cochran, Alastair, and John Stobbs. *The Search for the Perfect Swing* [reprinted]. Grass Valley (CA): The Booklegger, 1989.

Cook, Chuck. *Tips From the Tour*, New York: Golf Digest, 1986.

Cook, David L. "The Psychology of the Game." Presentation at the

First World Scientific Congress on Golf, St Andrews, Scotland, July 1990.

Coop, Richard H. "Concentration," *Golf Illustrated*, August 1990, pp. 28-40.

Coop, Richard H., with Bill Fields. *Mind Over Golf*. New York: Macmillan, 1993.

Cornish, Geoffrey S., and Ronald E. Whitten. *The Golf Course*. New York: The Rutledge Press, 1987.

Cox, Richard H. *Sports Psychology*. Dubuque (IA): William C. Brown, 1985.

Dennis, Larry. "The 45 Foot High," in *The 1991 U.S. Open Journal*, Hazeltine National Golf Club Events Publishing, New York: Golf Digest/Tennis, 1991, pp. 98-106.

Doak, Tom. *The Anatomy of a Golf Course*. New York: Lyons & Burford, Publishers, 1992.

Enhager, Kjell. *Quantum Golf*. New York: Warner Books, 1991.

Fine, Alan. *Mind Over Golf*. London: BBC Books, 1993.

Gallwey, W. Timothy, *The Inner Game of Golf*, New York: Random House, 1981.

Gilbert, Daniel T. "How Mental Systems Believe," *American Psychologist*, Vol. 46, No. 2, 1991, pp. 107-119.

Harris, Dorothy V., and Bette L. Harris. *Sports Psychology: Mental Skills for Physical People*. Champaign (IL): Leisure Press, 1984.

Hogan, Ben. *Five Lessons: The Modern Fundamentals of Golf*, New York: Simon & Schuster, 1957.

Hogan, Chuck. *Nice Shot* [videotape], Sedona (AZ): Sports Enhancement Associates, 1988.

Hunt, Morton. *The Universe Within*. New York: Simon & Schuster, 1982.

Iso-Ahola, Seppo E., and Brad Hatfield. *Psychology of Sports*, Dubuque (IA): William C. Brown, 1986.

Jacobs, Andrew A. *Sports Psychology: The Winning Edge in Sports* [videotape]. Kansas City (MO): The Winning Edge, 1988.

Keeler, O.B. and Grantland Rice, *The Bobby Jones Story*, Foulsham, London, 1990.

Lidz, Theodore. *The Person,*. New York: Basic Books, 1983.

Loehr, Jim. "Choking," New York: *World Tennis*, Feb. 1990, pp. 24-27.

Luria, Aleksandr R. *Higher Cortical Functions in Man*. (2nd ed.). New York: Basic Books, 1980.

Mackenzie, Marlin M. *Golf the Mind Game*. New York: Dell, 1990.

167

Mandell, Arnold J. "Golf and Psychotherapy, Man Against Himself: The Function of Theory Construction." Paper presented at the American Psychiatric Association, May 7-14, 1966.

Moore, Charles W. "The Mental Hazards of Golf," (1929), as in Thomas P. Stewart. *A Tribute to Golf*. Harbor Springs (MI): Stewart, Hunter and Assoc., Harbor Springs, 1990.

Morley, David C., "How To Conquer Fear and Anxiety on the Golf Course," New York: *Golf Digest*, August, 1976, pp. 73-78.

Nideffer, R. M. "The Relationship of Attention and Anxiety to Performance." In W. F. Straub (ed.), *Sports Psychology, An Analysis of Athlete Behavior* (2nd ed.). Ithaca (NY): Mouvement, 1980.

Ostrow, Andrew C. (ed.). *Directory of Psychological Tests in the Sport and Exercise Sciences*. Morgantown (WV): Fitness Information Technology, 1990.

Pace, Roy. *Target Golf*. Los Angeles: The Body Press, 1986.

Penick, Harvey. *Little Red Book*. New York: Simon & Schuster, 1992.

Restak, Richard M. *The Mind*. New York: Bantam Books, 1988.

Rhoads, James L. *The Hacker's Golf Guide*. San Diego: Cloverleaf Golf Publishing Co., 1991.

Rotella, Robert J., and Linda K. Bunker. *Mind Mastery for Winning Golf*. Englewood Cliffs (NJ): Prentice-Hall, 1981.

Rubenstein, Lorne. *Links, An Exploration into the Mind, Heart, and Soul of Golf*. Rocklin (CA): Prima Publishing, 1991.

Sanders, Vivien. *The Golfing Mind*. New York: Atheneum, 1988.

Singer, Robert N. "Thought Processes and Emotions in Sport," *The Physician and Sportsmedicine*, Vol. 10, No. 7, July 1982, pp. 75-88.

Tutko, Thomas, and Umberto Tosi. *Sports Psyching*. Los Angeles: J.P. Tarcher, 1976.

Wade, Don, and staff. "How to Concentrate for 18 Holes," New York: *Golf Digest*, March 1981, pp. 53-58.

Weiner, B., D. Russell, and D. Lerman. "The Cognitive-emotion process in achievement-related contexts," Journal of Personality and Social Psychology 37, 1211-20, 1979.

Williams, Jean M. (ed.). *Applied Sport Psychology*. Mountain View (CA): Mayfield Publishing, 1986.

Wiren, Gary, and Richard Coop. *The New Golf Mind*. New York: Simon & Schuster, 1978.

Wiren, Gary. *The PGA Manual of Golf*. New York: Macmillan, 1991.

Zaichkowsky, Leonard D., and C. Zvi Fuchs (eds.). *The Psychology of Motor Behavior*. Ithaca (NY): Mouvement Publications, 1986.

INDEX

INDEX